Chil
Great Depression

Growing Up in Cadillac Michigan During a Troubled Time

A LIFE STORY BY:
CLIFF "TOP" SJOGREN

FIRST EDITION: FEBRUARY 2016
SECOND EDITION: DECEMBER 2016

ISBN: 978-1-944786-32-8

COVER:
DOWNTOWN CADILLAC, C.1930S
COURTESY OF THE
WEXFORD COUNTY HISTORICAL SOCIETY, CADILLAC.
AUTHOR AS A CHILD, PERSONAL COLLECTION

PUBLISHER
CADILLAC PRINTING COMPANY, INC.
CADILLAC, MICHIGAN 49601

BOOKS AVAILABLE AT:
(231) 775-2488
orders@cadillacprintingco.com

Copyright © Clifford Frank Sjogren, Jr.

DEDICATION

I dedicate *Child of the Great Depression* to my wife, Patricia, our four children and their spouses, Stephen (Martha,) Janice, Sue (Stephen,) and Sigurd (Nancy,) and our grandchildren; Justin, Wesley, Andrew, Jacob, Brita, Peter, Claire, and William. They make me proud.

ACKNOWLEDGEMENTS

This book would never have happened without the strong support of my family. My parents led by example. Mom and Dad gave me a long leash and knew when to tug it back a bit. I learned many of life's important lessons as a child.

My thoughtful wife and our four children all deserve credit for my modest achievements. They tolerated my active participation in many outside work and organizational activities. My family gave me the unconditional love and support that enabled me to be professionally successful.

Others who toiled intelligently to make this story happen included my daughter-in-law Martha Wood Sjogren. Her sharp and thoughtful suggestions improved the piece immeasurably. Pamela Welliver, good friend and a publication design professional, edited the manuscript, managed the production, and offered valuable suggestions.

TABLE OF CONTENTS

	Page
DEDICATION and ACKNOWLEDGEMENTS	ii
FORWARD and PREFACE	vii

PART ONE: COMING OF AGE

A LIFE-DEFINING EXPERIENCE	1
A LIFE STORY	3
My Primary Family	7
Grandparents	14
My Home Town	19
My Home and Neighborhood	22
Learning Life's Lessons	25
Depression Era Meals	27
My Childhood Clothing	32
My Toy Box	35
Piano Lessons	38
Neighborhood Clubs	39
Boy Scouts	40
Cadillac School Camp (Torenta)	41
A Swedish Christmas Celebration	44
The Woods	46
Family Automobiles	48
Growing Up During a Troubled	52
Cooley Grade School	55
Sports and Games	59

TABLE OF CONTENTS

	Page
Sport Venues: Then and Now	63
A Special Aunt and Uncle	69
Cousin Bob and the Eagle School	70
Cadillac High School and the "Y"	73
Cadillac Youth Recreation Assoc.	79
Cadillac During the War Years	84
Employment During My School	87
Central Michigan College of Education	90
Alpine Skiing	92
Jack, My Best Friend	94
Jail Time	97
"Jack .. Why"	99

PART TWO: MOVING ON

US Navy Service	105
Courtship and Marriage	112
Teacher, Coach, & Camp Director	119
Frankfort High School	119
Cadillac Junior High School	120
Cadillac School Camp Director	121
Graduate School at Michigan	123
Harbor Springs High School	125

TABLE OF CONTENTS

	Page
A COLLEGE ADMISSIONS CAREER	126
Western Michigan University	127
The University of Michigan	131
University of Southern California	137
International Travel	141
Professional Organizations	143
Selected Publications Authored	148
MEMORABLE ADVENTURES	150
Murder in Key West (1949)	150
The Guns of Zamboanga (1965)	151
Flight Over the Kalahari (1966)	153
Clandestine Adventure in Lagos	159
Climbing Huayna Picchu (1971)	161
Navigating Check-Point Charlie	163
Nine Countries in Eleven Days	164
Unintended Heroics (1976)	166
Ski Iran (1977)	166
Skiing at La Parva in the Andes (1978)	168
Shaving Cream Applied in Amman (1984)	169
Carpet Purchases in Lahore (1985)	170
New York, New York, My Kind of Town	172

TABLE OF CONTENTS

Page

Visiting East Asia in a Private Jet (1992)	175
An Airman Turns Submariner (1993)	176

PART THREE: RETIREMENT

Traverse City	178
Cadillac	179
Detroit Turkey Trots (2013, 2015, 2016)	182
National Volunteer Activities	183
Local Volunteer Activities	184
Concluding Statement	188

APPENDICES

One:	Family Histories	189
Two:	Countries Visited	204
Three:	Employments	206
Four:	Residences	208
Five:	Autos Owned	212
Six:	Vita	214
Seven:	My Activity History	221

FORWARD

My cruise through life has been filled mostly with pleasant experiences and memories. My family and the countless thousands of individuals that I have encountered along the way deserve much of the credit for what I have accomplished.

My rather lengthy life adventure has resulted in some interesting numbers. Below are listed a few:

- a) Twenty-eight residences at which mail was received.
- b) Twenty-nine significant paid work experiences, six of which were "career track" (high school teaching and university admissions.)
- c) Three college degrees (BS, Central Michigan University; MA and PhD, The University of Michigan)
- d) More than a hundred foreign countries visited, many several times.
- e) Twenty-seven years as an International Baccalaureate of North America Board of Directors member.
- f) One national professional organization presidency.
- g) Fifty states visited.
- h) Twenty-two cars owned (fifteen purchased new.)
- i) Runs conquered at about thirty-five Alpine ski areas distributed over four continents.
- j) Three Rotary International memberships.
- k) Four children
- l) Eight grandchildren.
- m) One spouse.

While this book includes highlights of my college years, military service, and career, its major emphasis is on my coming of age during an important 20-year period of our nation's history. Between my birth in 1928 and my enlistment in the US Navy in 1948, American lives were profoundly influenced by worldwide turmoil resulting from the Great Depression (1929 to 1941) and World War II (1941 to 1945.) Life's lessons learned during that tumultuous period prepared me well for what was to come; a very happy life filled with love, good health, and countless pleasant and highly satisfying experiences.

A clarification is in order! Because this life story was written for our children and grandchildren, little has been written about them. After some sales success of my first non-career related publication, "Timber Town Tales," friends and family suggested that there might be some interest in my life story among a wider readership. (Some readers will note that parts of two or three stories in that book appear here.)

The process of writing "Child of the Great Depression," has rewarded me with many pleasant recollections. It has been said that writing about one's early life is reliving it! Thus, one might suggest that this task has thrust me nicely into my second childhood.

Generations Compared

The years from 1929 to 1941 were very difficult for most Americans. The Great Depression led to bank failures, severe unemployment, and huge entitlement programs that were necessary to prevent millions from dying of starvation. Even with several government funded employment programs such as the Works Progress Administration and the Civilian Conservation Corps, our area suffered a 25% unemployment rate.

Born in 1928 I remember well my coming of age during those Great Depression years. Having not lived during the "roaring twenties," I did not know that we existed under financial hardship. While adults suffered, most young children of that time lived happily.

I was raised as an average boy in an average family. The majority of Cadillac families those days were in most ways much like mine!

(*Before I proceed, an explanation is in order. I frequently apply the Pareto Principle when making distribution generalizations. Examples might be an educated guess that 20% of the workers produce 80% of the work, or 80% of the applicants to a university will require only 20% of staff processing time, or 80% of the problems are caused by 20% of the people. The Principle provides for exceptions to the rule.*)

Although children of my generation grew up during the Great Depression we were spared most of the personal struggles faced by today's young folks. Those who are coming of age now must adjust to the sometimes-destructive onslaught on our cultural values by the Internet, television, movies, and smart phones. Today, the ever-present media and social networks are constantly in the face of those sometimes too young to understand its impact on their lives! Many if not most of today's school-aged children will spend untold hours of their free time watching television, texting, tweeting, and face booking.

My generation used that time developing our life skills by organizing and playing adult-free games in churchyards, exploring the neighborhood, reading books, assisting parents with household chores, and communicating eye to eye. When bored, we would unleash our creative skills and seek new interests.

During the 1930's and 1940's my elementary school teachers placed a high priority on the four essential elements of good communication: Reading, Writing, Speaking, and Listening. My professional and personal life has been enriched greatly by my continued determination to strengthen my skills in those crucial areas.

Today, digitized shortcuts are replacing thoughtful and well-mannered written communications. Political debates and media discussions display flawed language skills and extreme rudeness. Candidates and TV staff and guests face each other as both speak at the same time while the volume of their voices increase.

Our media during the 1930's and 1940's was the local newspaper and a few radio programs that provided news, clean comedy, adventure stories, and music. We also had the ten-cent Saturday triple-feature movies where our heroes fought the bad guys and always won usually without the display of spilled blood.

Families worried about unemployment and health, knew and assisted their neighbors, and enjoyed their community. Most children did not want to disappoint their parents in any way. When told to do something, we usually did it without comment.

While I grew up during one of the most difficult periods in our country's history, I remain convinced that preparation for life was more complete while much less stressful compared to the challenges faced by children today. It was a simpler time.

Finally, as I look back on my life I find that various shades of the colors blue and gold represent four significant influences on my character that have led to my becoming the person I am today: My Swedish heritage (blue and golden yellow flag,) Cadillac High School (blue and gold,) US Navy (blue and gold,) and The University of Michigan (blue and maize.) I'm not sure what that trivia portends, but I found it rather interesting. Not coincidently, this book's cover is yellow and blue!

I have tried to live my life in a manner suggested by John H. Rhodes who penned:

> *"Do more than exist, live,*
> *Do more than touch, feel.*
> *Do more than look, observe.*
> *Do more than read, absorb.*
> *Do more than hear, listen.*
> *Do more than listen, understand.*
> *Do more than think, ponder.*
> *Do more than talk, say something."*
>
> ~ John H. Rhodes

PREFACE

OUR ANCESTORS COME TO AMERICA

Why America? What motivates people to move from their traditional homes and familiar surroundings to a new way of life in a faraway land? Is it restlessness? Adventurism? Economic improvement? Freedom from restrictive government and religious influences? Escapism? To be with family and friends? I suspect that it was one or more of those factors that inspired my paternal and maternal grandparents to leave their homes in Sweden and Canada to seek a new life in America.

Understanding the economic and political conditions in Sweden will provide an appreciation of what might have motivated the families Sjögren and Eriksson to settle in their new land.

During the latter part of the 19th century, Sweden was a land in transition. The agrarian tradition of the country was giving way to worldwide industrialization. In Scandinavia and elsewhere, the lure of money brought about by this economic revolution drew young families from their rural homes to large urban centers.

Sweden, a land of traditional orderliness and a strong sense of family values and cohesiveness, underwent tumultuous change as its citizens sought the better life.

The Lutheran church (Lutheranism was the state religion) and the federal government applied strict controls on its populations during the late 19th century. One was expected to practice mostly unwritten codes of behavior. Loyalty to the church and the state were demanded. Individualism and creativity were discouraged. It was a stifling environment and restlessness was rampant, particularly among the young and idealistic.

Under those circumstances, one of two options existed for the more restless citizens. One would either help bring about change in the way things were done, which would require some type of forceful or passive rebellious action or one would leave the country.

During the late 19th century large numbers of Scandinavians opted for the latter. Many decided to seek their fortunes and unleash their boundless energies in America. Countless descendants of those adventurous Swedes owe their American lives to their ancestors' decisions to sail west. Among their destinations were the thriving lumber producing areas located in the sparsely settled northwestern part of Michigan's Lower Peninsula.

In April 1894, my Grandfather, Frans Sjögren, departed the Swedish Baltic Sea island of Gotland for Michigan. At about the same time Ida Maria Eriksson departed the Swedish mainland with her aunt and uncle for Ludington, Michigan. The descendants of those new Americans will be forever grateful for whatever happened to bring these two intelligent and interesting personalities together in their new land.

The translation of the name, Sjögren, combines two common Swedish terms. *Sjö* means "lake" or "sea" or "body of water." *Gren* is "branch." One might logically assume, therefore, that our early family members had some association with the nautical trades. Indeed, they did as they were islanders. Among my paternal ancestors is at least one ship captain.

My father and his seven siblings, all born in timber harvest areas within 50 miles of Cadillac, Michigan, were raised in a Swedish-speaking home with its Swedish culture and behaviors. Family-centered Swedish traditions were carried on for future generations.

Grandfather Frans Sjögren worked in the timber harvest areas of Baldwin, Thompsonville, Jennings, and Cadillac. His primary employers during his early life were the Cobbs and Mitchell and Mitchell Brothers lumber companies. He was also employed by the Acme vehicle manufacturers.

Unfortunately, we know less about my mother's ancestry. Rye Gould and Elizabeth Worden were born in Plainfield, Ontario and married in Bay City, Michigan in 1888. After several years and the birth of four children in Rosebush, they moved to Cadillac during the 1890's where Rye took an office worker position with the Cobbs and Mitchell Company.

The early Worden's were apparently a well-to-do European family of mixed French and Dutch ancestry.

My Grandmother Elizabeth, daughter of William Worden had a letter written in 1912 to her uncle J. E. Warden from his aunt. In part, it read: "*Grandmother Ouelette, from Paris, France, was of a noble family and had to flee to England. The Great Grandfather was Earl of Lorraine. Great Grandmother was Lady Margaret. She married Sir John Francis. The name 'Ouelette' was then called 'Willett.'*"

After a few Worden family members settled in Ontario, they had a brother in Holland send his wife to New York with their jewels and money. She never arrived as the boat was shipwrecked. Later other family members left Holland for Ontario.

My mother, the last of Rye and Elizabeth's five children, was born in Cadillac on February 1, 1905. Soon after she married Dad, she embraced the Swedish culture and the many Nordic traditions the Sjögrens held dear. Her Swedish meal preparation at Christmas time is legendary within the Sjögren clan.

Pat, my wife of 62 years is also proud to be a "Swedish American." Her birth mother's maiden name was Flodquist.

Both paternal and maternal grandparents were fine people with interesting family histories. Why Mom and Dad embraced the cultural values and life styles that mostly resembled Swedish rather than that of the Dutch / French culture remains a mystery to me. My cousins generally seemed to follow the pattern set by Frans and Ida which has been especially noticeable at

Christmastime although some separation seems to be happening during the generation of my children.

We are a land created and populated by immigrants from all over who brought their rich cultures and new ways of doing things to the American shores. Let us always welcome our new residents and learn from them.

Sweden: Yellow on light blue   Canada: Red on white

PART I: COMING OF AGE

A LIFE-DEFINING EXPERIENCE

*Do not call any work menial until
you have watched a proud person do it.*
~ Robert Brault

It was summer 1953. I had married Pat Chick on June 20 and looked forward to my senior year at Central Michigan College of Education.

The previous fall I was honorably discharged from the US Navy where I served four years as an aerial photographer. I found that a Lansing aerial photography company was one of a very few in Michigan. I applied for a position and was told that I had the experiences they needed and that I would be hired. Unintentionally, I neglected to tell them that I wanted summer work only. Their response when later told was a simple "sorry!"

Early in my life my parents instilled in me the confidence to make decisions. I was quite sure that I should delay my return to college and take the fulltime job offer where I could use my aerial photography skills and make a lot of money. I knew that Pat would understand.

Before the "sorry" response Pat and I had sub-let a small apartment in a temporary housing facility on campus at Michigan State College. As we would be in Lansing for the summer, Pat suggested that we delay the aerial photography job decision for a few weeks. Although my decision had been challenged, I reluctantly agreed. I landed a seasonal position at the huge Oldsmobile assembly plant in Lansing.

In a structure, at least the size of two football fields, a partially completed 1954 Oldsmobile rolled by my workstation on the conveyer track about every 45 seconds. As one of four line workers, my assignment was every fourth car. I had less than three minutes to slip into the passenger seat with a nine-pound heater, kick it up under the glove compartment, and hold it in place with my left foot while I attached it to the firewall with seven screws.

Because the plant line managers felt that a good worker could handle the assignment in a little over two minutes, another task was added. I had to exit the rolling vehicle, quickly exchange my power screwdriver for a small tool, and remove two jet screws from the passenger side windshield wiper. It was very stressful work.

After my first day on the job, my thoughtful co-workers invited me to join them for a beer at the tavern across the street from the plant. They seemed like nice fellows and I wanted to know them better. Alas! After two or three days of conversations about either the Detroit Tigers or "the line" and the people who made the cars, I was bored. I politely refused future invitations to join them in their late afternoon pleasures.

Fortunately, the company staff cared about its employee's health. After a few weeks of repeated strain on some leg and back muscles, I was re-assigned to installing taillight housings on the moving vehicles, a much less stressful task.

That life-defining experience came quite unexpectedly. With Pat's encouragement and the assembly line experience at Oldsmobile, I decided for the first time in my life to take my education seriously and earn my degree.

I also learned that family-shared decision-making will usually lead to better decisions! At least four major decisions during our married life resulted from Pat's gentle persuasion to retreat from my preferences and move on to a location that would better serve the family. My rather selfish interests in skiing, hunting, and fishing were giving way to better opportunities for our family. Those moves were Cadillac to Ann Arbor in 1957 for my MA degree; Harbor Springs to Kalamazoo in 1960 for a position at Western Michigan University; Kalamazoo to Ann Arbor in 1964 for a position at The University of Michigan; and Traverse City to Pasadena, California in 1989 for a position at USC.

We were in full agreement for our final move, Traverse City to Cadillac in 2001.

"Work hard, work smart, and have fun doing it" is an adage I crafted for myself many years ago. Those few words have served me well as I carried out my career and volunteer responsibilities. I got the first part right at the Oldsmobile factory job. I just didn't "have fun doing it!"

A LIFE STORY

I think I've discovered the secret of life - you just hang around until you get used to it.
~ Charles Schulz

This is my life story. It describes some experiences of a lad born in 1928 and coming of age in a unique and dynamic period of our country's history: The Great Depression and the World War II years. Our family, as most others during the 1930's, struggled to keep food on the table and heat in the home.

I was then too young to realize that we were poor. I was kept warm and well fed and enjoyed a fun-filled early childhood. As a teenager during the war years of the 1940's, I learned the value of sacrificing for a greater cause.

The life lessons I learned during those turbulent years of the depression and the war served me well during the ensuing decades of a full and productive life.

Both sets of my grandparents emigrated from foreign lands and settled in my hometown of Cadillac, Michigan during the late 1890's. Their decisions to live in that remarkable community have had a profound influence on my character. The essentials of my life were molded as I made my way to adulthood in Northern Michigan.

As was true with both my personal and professional life, the trek from my childhood home at 723 Wood Street (now South Mitchell Street) to our last retirement home at 7774 Mackinaw Trail on Cadillac's south end, featured some rather steep albeit pleasant inclines, a plateau, and no major declines. That path headed south up a steep slope to the beautiful Maple Hill Cemetery followed by a long hill to the highest point in the area. There one could view in the distance a pleasant lake, a variety of hills, and thousands of acres of hardwood and pine forests.

In my early days, Mom, Dad, and I would squeeze into the family 1928 Model A Ford coupe and make our way to the top of that Mackinaw Trail hill to view sunsets and approaching thunderstorms. How could I have imagined that my retirement home would occupy the very site where I as a child enjoyed family togetherness, both literally and figuratively?

During the Great Depression years, I learned important life lessons on Wood Street and its adjacent areas. The neighborhood was nicely nestled between hills on the south and east, a beautiful lake on the west, and a vibrant community on the north. Within a few minutes' walk I could visit both sets of grandparents, favorite aunts and uncles, and many friends. Much was learned from family and friends that has served me well

My family purchased from Mom's parents our three-apartment home in late 1931. Wood Street, while tree-lined, was not a particularly attractive street. Gas stations, automobile repair shops, a giant mill, and other commercial establishments were mixed in amongst the modest homes. Windows in those homes rattled as southbound trucks releasing their heavy black smoke began a determined and very noisy acceleration to reach the top of Cemetery Hill, about three blocks distant.

My parents were married in Cadillac on August 18, 1925. In 1927 or early 1928, the couple moved to Detroit, where Dad's first job was mechanical drafting for the Continental Motor Company. There was money to be made in Detroit and workers from all over the country moved there to improve their lot in life.

After Dad's parents also moved to Detroit, he and his father became painting contractors. Dad's parents did not care for the big city and soon returned to Cadillac while Dad and Mom remained in Detroit where he continued as a painter.

I was born on June 30, 1928 in Highland Park Hospital near Detroit. Interestingly, both Pat Chick, who would later become my wife, and Jack Quinn, my best high school friend, were also born in that hospital.

The following year, the stock markets plunged, banks went broke, and countless Americans lost their savings and jobs.

Our family returned to its roots in Cadillac in 1930. We moved into a small farmhouse on Boon Road west of the airport with Mom's sister, Pearl Hillard, her husband Will, and their beagle, Duke. Dad joined his father as a painter and decorator.

After a few months, we moved to our permanent home on Wood Street. Why was it named Wood Street? Maybe it was because of the many maple trees that lined the brick-surfaced street or was it the huge Cobbs and Mitchell sawmill and flooring plant that was but a short block from my home? Most likely it was the countless logs that had to be laid side by side before a road to uptown could be constructed over the large wetland.

Sigurd Paul, my only sibling, was born on April 1, 1935 in Cadillac.

My early years were filled with happiness. My childhood lacked the meanness, fear, hostility, loneliness and health and family problems that occasionally afflicted young people. I had the advantage of loving parents, a small-town environment, a close-knit family, and a close-by extended family. We never had much money but we enjoyed a rich life.

By any measurement, Mom and Dad were ideal parents. If all children could be raised and nurtured through the many stages of their early development as were Sig and I, the world would be a much more pleasant place to live, work, and enjoy. Their devotion to their family made the move from the deep depression years of the 1930s into and beyond the war years of the 1940s, a memorable and pleasant experience for my brother and me.

In 1946, a year after the war ended I graduated from Cadillac High School and began the transition to adulthood. Four years each of college and US Navy service prepared me well for a professional career as a teacher, coach, college administrator, consultant, and many years of professional and community volunteer service.

When Patricia, my dear wife of 63 years and counting, began experiencing serious cognitive issues we sold our retirement home and moved into a condominium on the south shore of Lake Cadillac, about two blocks from my childhood home and a mere 30 feet from my old swimming hole. Soon after, Pat was entered into the Curry House, a local memory care facility.

Now at age 88, I reflect back on a life that has been both ordinary and unusual in many ways. I hope that you will enjoy my story.

MY PRIMARY FAMILY

*My father didn't tell me how to live;
he lived, and let me watch him do it.*
~ Clarence Budinton Kelland

DAD: My father, Clifford ("Cap") Frans Gustav Sjogren, was born in Jennings on June 6, 1901, the third of Ida and Frans' eight children. It was soon after the Mitchell Brothers Lumber Corporation relocated the young family from Cadillac to Jennings.

Reared by Swedish parents, Dad could not converse in English until after he was enrolled in the local school at the age of five.

The family returned to Cadillac in 1908. After completing grade ten and earning recognition as a mechanical drawing student at Cadillac High School, Dad quit school and worked at assorted jobs. He delivered bread baked by the Johnson and Kaiser Grocery and Bakery to area stores and later worked at the St. John's Table Company.

In 1919 Dad enlisted in the US Army Air Corps, where he served as a draftsman at an air base. After his discharge, he became a draftsman for the Kent County Road Commission

As a young child during the Great Depression, I remember Dad as a hard- working painter and paperhanger. Because he was a good and honest craftsman he seemed always to have work. He would return home, often after dark, in his white, paint-spattered work clothes, clean up his brushes and equipment, and retire to his comfortable chair by the radio to listen to the day's news while he waited for supper.

He kept his frustrations experienced during the day's labor to himself and always greeted my return from school, athletic practice, or work with a smile and a readiness to listen to a recap of my activities.

I never heard him utter a negative word about a person's economic level, race, or religion. While he would never curse in English, he and his brothers would sometimes converse in Swedish with childish grins and an unwillingness to translate their words.

He loved to hunt and fish. He was a serious environmentalist well before the term was popular. My brother Sig and I were always told to "leave the woods a little cleaner than when you entered." Most of his deer hunting trips with his friends to the Upper Peninsula saw him carting a camera rather than a rifle. "I am not mad at the deer," he insisted. "Why shoot them?"

The entire family enjoyed fishing. Dad always had a boat of some kind. We would fish lakes Cadillac and Mitchell, labeled at that time as Little Lake and Big Lake, as well as many other area lakes. On one of our fishing trips to a Missaukee County lake, we rescued an elderly man who had spent the night on the bottom of his overturned anchored boat

During the mid-1940s, Dad constructed a houseboat that was the talk of Cadillac. It was about 24 feet by 10 feet and could sleep four comfortably. When the shades were closed, one could lift the tabletop and view the lake's bottom and the fish that would swim by. The boat was always at anchor somewhere on Lake Cadillac for the entire summer. It was a fun place to entertain friends during my teenage years.

Dad served as Excellent High Priest for the Royal Arch Masons and was Worshipful Master of Clam Lake Lodge #331, Free and Accepted Masons. On October 23, 1971, the Lodge honored him for his many years of service and dedication to the Masonic craft. He had been treasurer since 1964. He also served as an officer in the Parent-Teacher Association of the Cadillac Public Schools.

As I grew older, I began to appreciate the freedom I had as a child. Dad and Mom gave Sig and me a lengthy leash and as long as we stayed out of trouble, it would not be pulled back. That parenting style served as an important motivation for me. I was not required to be home or be in bed at a certain time. I was free to make my own decisions and I learned how to make the right ones (usually!). I chose my friends, determined how to spend my allowance or earnings, selected my clothes to wear, and decided whether or not to attend Sunday school and church services. I learned responsibility by having it thrust upon me at an early age and the confidence I developed during those days served me well later in life.

During the 1960's after about 25 years in business, Dad completed his career as owner and manager of Cap's Paint Store, located in the other ground floor apartment of our South Mitchell Street home. With Mom's help, he had managed a very successful business. He was one of the few paint retailers in Cadillac who had a lengthy experience in the trade.

Among Dad's paint suppliers were Congressman (and later president) Gerald Ford's parents who supplied Dad with his Hooker-brand paints from his Grand Rapids paint supply business. The Fords would plan their business trips to Cadillac for early October and enjoy Mom's homemade biscuits and coffee followed by a color tour of the area with their hosts.

Trying to classify Dad's political orientation is difficult. His trusting nature took a hit when the conversation turned to politics. He would usually vote for the most conservative candidate although he seemed to be less than enthusiastic about any element of government that tried to manipulate the life styles of ordinary folks.

President Franklin D. Roosevelt was disliked by Dad because of the many federal entitlement programs he initiated to assist families during the Great Depression. Interestingly, while Dad was opposed to the Works Progress Administration he looked favorably on the Civilian Conservation Corps both of which were designed to address the unemployment problems. The preservation of the forests surrounding his hometown was always high among Dad's interests.

He was a very good Dad. I feel fortunate to have grown to adulthood under his and Mom's guidance

*I love my mother as the trees love
water and sunshine – She helps me grow,
prosper, and reach great heights.
~ Terri Guillemets*

MOM: Among the notes from Mom and Dad's family history scrapbook is the following poignant entry penned by Mom: "*He first noticed his future wife . . . as she waited at the curb for him to drive up Howard Street. She smiled at him. It is strange how often he happened to be at that corner soon after school was out and she was going home.*"

It is not unusual for men to praise their mothers. By nature, and by love those remarkable women brought us into the world, kept us warm, well fed, clean, and out of harm's way.

Moms made sure that we learned the good lessons of life before releasing us to the world some two decades later. Even in her later years my mom continued her wise counsel and love. Dads, as well, had their special role in the child's life, but while they were "protecting, hunting, and gathering," to keep the family alive, moms stayed home to nurture the children during those crucial years of their lives. My mom and dad could have been the poster folks for that parental model.

My mother, the youngest in a family of five children, was born of Ontario immigrant parents on February 1, 1905 in Cadillac. She graduated from Cadillac High School in 1923. Mom was very close to her sister, Pearl, who also lived in Cadillac. Brother Elgie served in World War One and settled in Ann Arbor where he was a barber near the University of Michigan stadium. Morley also moved to Ann Arbor and Ward settled in Albuquerque.

While going to high school, Mom worked Saturdays and vacations at the Woolworth Five and Ten Cent Store in downtown Cadillac. After graduation, she became the "office girl" for the Leslie-Johnson Electric Company. Soon after, she accepted a job as secretary with the Webber-Ashworth Furniture Company, located at 106 South Mitchell Street. In memory of Mom (and other reasons!) I sometimes visit that address to enjoy a glass of Logger's Daughter, a fine beer crafted on site.

Mom was the textbook stay-at-home housewife and mother who also loved the outdoors and extended family functions of all kinds. She was never one to raise her voice in anger. Mom shared with Dad all of the responsibilities of home management and child rearing. She never complained.

Mom was the best fisherperson in the family. While Dad and I changed our bait often and swirled our poles masterfully to attract the prey, Mom sat patiently until the big one took her worm.

She loved the October small game hunting trips with Aunt Pearl and Uncle Will where she and her sister would prepare and display the lunch on a blanket on the forest floor to await the return of the hunters. In the meantime, she would gather pine knots for the wood-burning stove back home. She and Dad would frequently retrieve and dispose of trash left by thoughtless forest visitors.

Mom would always be able to scrape up a meal for the "hobos," a 1930's term for the homeless men who rode the rails from town to town. They would sit on the back porch to enjoy their soup or sandwich and usually offer to do some work to pay for the meal. They were very polite and appreciative of Mom's generosity and were never a problem. She even had repeat "customers!" When I would return home from school or play, these men would greet me warmly and move off the steps as I made my entrance into the kitchen. I envied their carefree existence and their constant travel.

In 1940, Mom joined the Goodwill Chapter #425 of the Eastern Star. In January 1946, she was installed as the Grand Warder of the Grand Chapter of the Michigan Eastern Star, one of only 18 state officers in the organization. Because of Dad's business commitments, I was invited to accompany Mom on her inauguration at Detroit's Masonic Temple. Garbed in a tuxedo and painfully uncomfortable black, shiny shoes and with Mom's arm locked in mine, I nervously escorted her to the elevated head table where my teenage dining behaviors would be on display for a very large and sophisticated crowd. As was her usual manner, however, Mom described the experience and my participation in it as a most positive affair in every way. Mom also served as an officer in the Cadillac chapter of the Business and Professional Women's Organization.

Mom assisted Dad with the management of Cap's Paint Store from the mid-nineteen forties until they retired from the business in the 1960's. She was the bookkeeper and served customers while Dad did the heavy work and consulted with clients on decorating issues. The business was highly successful and provided my parents with a financially comfortable retirement.

Mom never uttered a negative word or phrase about another person! She defined "political correctness" by talking about friends, acquaintances, and public personalities without sarcasm or demeaning statements. She embodied John Gardner's classic statement that reads, "People who meet friendly people wherever they go do much to create that friendliness." She seemed to like and respect everybody and that feeling seemed always to be mutual.

The dreadful Alzheimer's disease eventually claimed Mom's life at age 78. Dad, Mom's ever-attendant caretaker and in very good health at age 82, died suddenly three months later. He had lost the love of his life from which he was unable or unwilling to recover.

A brother is a friend given by Nature.
~ Jean Baptiste Legouve

SIGURD PAUL: My brother and only sibling, Sig, was well liked by everybody. Sigurd Paul Sjogren was born April 1, 1935 in Cadillac. He possessed Mom's engaging smile, quiet demeanor, and was soft-spoken and intelligent. He had many of Dad's mechanical and building skills and was always eager to help his family and friends in any way. I was seven years older than Sig.

Because of his good looks and consistently friendly demeanor, I did not mind having him tag along with me to the youth center or the beach where I joined my many friends for our mid-teenage activities. Those friends of mine, mostly of the female gender, admired Sig as I looked on with pride. His favorite sports were skiing and sailing, both of which take full advantage of nature's forces without seriously disturbing the environment. He nicely mastered both sports.

Sig served his country honorably in the US Army where he was an instructor of the ski troops. Most of his military career was spent in the mountains of Alaska.

After graduating with a business degree from Central Michigan University, Sig was employed by two or three large companies before returning to Cadillac to work for Williams Sporting Goods. He ended his working career as purchasing manager at the Cadillac Rubber and Plastics Company, eventually bought by Avon Corp., of England.

Sig married Melissa Tornberg of Cadillac in October 1966. They have two children, Anders and Brita, both University of Michigan Engineering College graduates and highly successful in their careers.

My brother and I never had a serious "falling out." He was always there for me when I sought his assistance or counsel. Sig died in Cadillac June 11, 2012.

Sig often made me wish that I had more siblings.

GRANDPARENTS

Nobody can do for little children what grandparents do. Grandparents sort of sprinkle stardust over the lives of little children.
~ Alex Haley

Both of my Sjogren grandparents were larger in stature than my Gould grandparents; hence, I assigned them the "big" and "little" designations. Both sets of grandparents lived in Cadillac and I visited them often.

Mom's parents, "Little" grandma, Margaret Elizabeth (Lib) Worden Gould, born in Ontario of mixed UK, French and Dutch heritage and "Little Grandpa," George Ryerson "Rye" Gould, also of Ontario, moved to Michigan and took up residence in Bay City, Belding, and Rosebush before settling in Cadillac. Rye was a long-time employee of the Cobbs and Mitchell Lumber Company in Cadillac. Once in Belding, and again in Cadillac, Rye attempted to make a living as a storeowner and operator, but failed on both attempts. Rye was employed as a member of the Cobbs and Mitchell clerical staff.

    Grandma and Grandpa Sjogren's family history is more complete and no less interesting. "Big Grandma," Ida Eriksson, arrived in Ludington from Heby, Sweden with her aunt, uncle and sister Anna, in about 1892. Her father, Erik Eriksson, was a craftsman who made the iron entry gates for their Lutheran church in Heby, near Uppsala, Sweden.

    "Big Grandpa," Frans, made his way as a teenager to the Swedish mainland from his home in Hemse, on Gotland Island. From there he probably traversed Sweden to Goteborg where he caught a ship to Liverpool, England and sailed on to New York. Somehow he made his way to the Sisson-Lilley lumber camp, a few miles south of present day Baldwin, Michigan. Both of the Swedish families were good, hardworking citizens with Frans' family primarily farmers, shop owners, and seamen (one was a captain of a ship) while Ida's family were mostly craftsmen.

    "Big" Grandpa and Grandma met in Sisson – Lilley and were soon after married in Ludington. In the mid-1890s, Frans and Ida Sjogren moved to Thompsonville and then to Cadillac where Frans joined the huge Cobbs and Mitchell lumber operation as a woodsman and a painter. In 1899 or 1900, the small family moved about eight miles to the Mitchell Brothers mill town of Jennings. After about 10 years the family returned to Cadillac for the remainder of their lives.

    Each family displayed a set of characteristics that, while noticeably different from each other, lived by a proper set of principles and standards that influenced in a positive way their many descendants. Mom's side of the family was quietly introspective and gentlemanly and ladylike in every way. They were hard working, caring people. They all remained solidly in the middle-income population, as they became electricians, barbers, salesmen, mill workers, and craftsmen. While I am sure that they experienced the emotional ups and downs faced by most of us, they hid their feelings well. Displays of anger, overwhelming sadness, and uncontrollable laughter were rare, although Aunt Pearl's high-pitched sounds of joy at things both funny and not so funny were pleasurable and somewhat contagious.

Other than Aunt Pearl, the Gould's might best be described as folks who smile and frown rather than laugh out loud and cuss. Mom fit that mold perfectly! She reacted to my bad behavior with a tear in her eye and an ever so slight smile on her lips. When I did something to make her proud, it too, would elicit that slight smile and sometimes a tear or two.

The Sjogrens were quite different in their demeanor. When Grandma Sjogren first met Pat, soon to be my wife, she warned her that the Sjogrens unleashed their sometimes-warped sense of humor at just about any occasion. All of Grandma's eight children, as well as her fun-loving husband, enjoyed the jokes and the constant repartee during family events.

Grandma Sjogren trusted everybody. When it was suggested that she lock her home when she was away, she hung the key at eye level on the outside door casing "in case someone needed to get in!"

They were loyal to their Swedish Lutheran church and were disappointed when several of their descendants were less than enthusiastic about attending formal religious rites. All their offspring and spouses were successful in their careers. Among the Sjogrens were nurses, painters / decorators, a storeowner, and three industrialists, one of whom became the manager of a large tool steel company in

Detroit. Unlike the Gould's, when the Sjogrens were happy, sad, or angry, those around them knew it!

My grandparents, by action rather than words, were important elements in the development of my character. They were intelligent, hardworking, honest, and loyal to their new country and their family.

The worst four days in my young life began on Jan 8, 1940 when "Big Grandpa," Adolph Frans Fridolph Sjogren, died at age 65. Four days later, "Little Grandpa," George Ryerson Gould died at age 77. Until that miserable week, I had not experienced the death of a loved one. I was then eleven years old with 22 aunts and uncles, all in their first marriages, ten cousins, who were not only alive and well, but all were residents of Michigan.

My grandparents were very special people in my life. I hope that my grandchildren will remember me in similar ways.

18

*Ida / Frans Sjogren,
Grandparents*

*Elizabeth / Rye Gould,
Grandparents*

*Cap / Pauline Sjogren –
Parents c. 1925*

*Pauline / Cap Sjogren
c. 1960*

MY HOME TOWN

Freedom is not the right to live as we please but the right to find how we ought to live in order to fulfill our potential.
~ Ralph Waldo Emerson

Cadillac is an attractive lakeside town nestled in the forests and rolling hills of northwest Lower Michigan.

George Mitchell, a timber speculator, founded the Village of Clam Lake in 1871. The village was chartered as the City of Cadillac in 1877 and soon became an important timber harvesting and wood product-manufacturing center.

Soon after his arrival, Mitchell unleashed his considerable intelligence and compassion to plan a dynamic community on the shores of a beautiful lake. He set aside prime property for schools, churches, and parklands. At about the same time the Grand Rapids and Indiana Railway arrived in Clam Lake. The giant white pine trees could now be harvested and transported to markets throughout the U.S. and the world.

Much of the credit for Cadillac's emergence as a "can-do" community goes to the large number of Swedish immigrants who settled the area in the late 19th century. They brought with them timber-harvesting skills and a hands-on knowledge of how to make machines and tools for both harvesting and processing the timber. They crafted flooring, construction wood, furniture, and many other products needed by a growing nation. They were also a productive work force because of their experience in cold climates with shortened daylight hours during winter months.

Frans Sjogren, my paternal grandfather, and his new bride, Ida, were among those Swedes who settled in Cadillac in the 1890's.

The new community was often defined by superlatives. At times the community featured the largest flooring mill in the world, highest percentage of home ownership and the lowest percentage of unemployment in Michigan, and the world's largest manufacturing company that made tables exclusively. The early business tycoons, the Mitchells, Diggins', Cummers, and Cobbs' families, while highly successful as entrepreneurs, were quite unselfish, as well. They created parks and recreation areas, installed utility systems, built roadways, schools, the hospital, churches, and donated a beautiful site for the Maple Hill Cemetery.

One wonders how many children today are raised in an environment that is within walking distance of a very nice lake, many hills, thick forests, good snow and ice, and a lively downtown. I get restless when visiting family and friends in metropolitan suburbs.

Many Cadillac people have achieved national recognition for their achievements. As an example, Fred W. Green, while born in Manistee, grew up in Cadillac and graduated from Cadillac High School. He served as Governor of Michigan during the Great Depression. Governor Green was inducted into the Michigan Transportation Hall of Honor in 1992. The Michigan Department of Transportation Website (MDOT) includes the following:

"Clearly one of Michigan's "Good Roads" governors, Green enthusiastically supported expansion and upgrading the state highway system during his two terms as chief executive (1927-1931). He was the "inventor" of the yellow no-passing line, first used in Michigan, which eventually became a standard safety device on highways everywhere."

http://www.michigan.gov/mdot/0,4616,7-151-9623_11154-126455--,00.html

On that same site, MDOT reported that Cadillac native, A. L. (Lew) Burridge was known as "The Dean of Highway Engineers." Burridge was a close friend and colleague of Governor Green.

"CADILLAC, CITY OF QUALITY MADE POSSIBLE BY MEN OF VISION"
(Front page banner, Cadillac Evening News, 1940's)

View of Mitchel Street looking north

*Sketch by Fred H. Lamb.,
Courtesy Wexford County
Historical Society*

MY HOME AND NEIGHBORHOOD

A house is not a home unless it contains food and fire for the mind as well as the body.
~ Benjamin Franklin

Soon after his arrival, Cadillac's founder George Mitchell set aside prime property for schools, churches, and parklands. His unselfish contributions to his new community made Cadillac a special place for generations of residents.

As was true in most communities of those early years, many small businesses were located in residential areas. Within a short distance of my Wood (South Mitchell) Street home were several service stations that sold gasoline and repaired cars.

My neighborhood included three or four grocery markets, a bakery, a beauty shop, a barbershop, a dressmaking factory, the Michigan State Police post, and a funeral home. The Cobbs and Mitchell lumber mill was a block northwest of my home. A sawmill and an ice storage building were close by on the shore of Lake Cadillac. A girl's coat factory was a block north.

Our home consisted of three apartments. Two of them were always rented until one became the site of Cap's Paint Store, Dad's retail business that opened in the 1940's. The apartments were rented during the 1930's for five dollars a week, payable each Saturday.

The back yard featured a vegetable garden, lilac trees, some fruit trees, a little bit of lawn, and a small garage. One winter Dad speared a 40" pickerel and hung it in the garage overnight. Much to his chagrin, cats invaded the garage and left only a pile of fish bones. Dad soon after built a large, three-stall, cement block garage that was cat-proof.

A brick front porch with a swing faced the tree-lined Wood Street in the front of the house. Many evenings were spent on the front porch greeting strollers passing by and waving to the car passengers. We knew most of our neighbors and they were a friendly lot.

Our kitchen, a small twenty-foot square room at the rear of our home, harbored countless happy memories for me. At one corner was a pantry, well stocked with Mom's preserves, rows of canned goods, cooking supplies, bags of flour and sugar, and a large porcelain jug to hold our drinking water. One of my tasks about every other day was to carry two milk pails to the town water pump about a block up Cobbs street, prime the pump with a pint or two of water, and fetch the family's drinking supply.

One cold day, I pressed my tongue on the pump spout for a sip of water. There it stayed until an alert local lady noticed my problem and released me from the spout with a large cup of warm water. She was well qualified for the task as several children lived in the neighborhood.

A single dipper rested by the water jug in our pantry that was used by all family members.

I also emptied the melted water from the icebox. Ice was delivered to the homes on Wood Street by horse and buggy. The iceman, without knocking, would walk into the kitchen, usually with a cheery "Hello, Pauline" to announce his arrival and deposit a cake of ice in the icebox. We youngsters would use the occasion to pet his horse and look for chips of ice for our morning treats. We imagined that the horse enjoyed our presence as he or she was always smiling.

Dad bought a GE refrigerator with an eye-level label that read, "Presented to the Family, Christmas 1939." We were so proud of that magical machine.

When I arrived home from school for lunch on Mondays during wintertime, I was usually met with laundry hanging on lines strung every which way in the kitchen. After a little game of "peek-a-boo" with Mom, I would sit among the freshly cleaned linens and clothing enjoying a hot meal enriched by the sweet odor of newly laundered clothes.

The wash machine was located in a heated attached shed accessed through a kitchen door. In the shed was a trap door to the fruit cellar. The coal for our stoves was also piled in the shed. Coal was delivered through a window and coal dust was a continuing problem during winter. The living quarters, however, never showed evidence of coal dust from the adjacent shed. Mom was a superb housekeeper.

A large cooking stove in the kitchen provided warm meals and hot water for dish washing and bathing. A table and four chairs where we enjoyed our meals together rested near a window with a view of the yard.

Opposite the heating stove in the living room, was the family console radio around which the family would convene for our favorite radio shows including the Lone Ranger, Jack Armstrong, Buck Jones, and comedians, Jack Benny, Bob Hope, Red Skelton, and Amos and Andy. Mom's piano was always at the ready, where she entertained family and guests with the popular tunes of the period. Overstuffed chairs, a comfortable couch, and a bookcase were included in the room's furnishings.

Our two bedrooms were upstairs accessed from a rather long hallway that was a popular play area. Brother Sig and I occupied the front bedroom in separate beds and two dressers. There was little heat upstairs, but we adjusted to the cold. That experience served me well! To this day, I have a high level of tolerance for the cold. Mom and Dad slept in the back bedroom with its small walk-in closet.

Thank you George Mitchell for choosing this remarkable location for your town!

LEARNING LIFE'S LESSONS

I don't care how poor a man is;
if he has family, he's rich.
~ Dan Wilcox and Thad Mumford

Early days in Cadillac's south end were very special to me. We young folks passed the time by engaging in rather competitive sandlot football and softball games in the church yard, playing cowboys and Indians in Horseshoe Hollow, hiking in Brown's woods, exploring the mysteries of abandoned factories, the city dump, gravel pits, feasting on rhubarb and apples from neighborhood garden lots, skiing in Devil's Kettle in the Maple Hill Cemetery, and swimming and fishing in Lake Cadillac down by the old sawmill.

When boredom set in, I would approach the porch of one of my friends' homes with a loud "Hey, Harry, or Lloyd, or Fred," or any one of several boys who lived in the area. Girls came much later in my life! Children then would not think of bothering the parents by knocking on the door! Everybody's mom was a good cook and I was frequently rewarded with warm cookies and milk as I sought playmates.

While none of the families in our neighborhood was well off financially during those years of the Great Depression, they all seemed to get by. Fathers who were fortunate enough to be employed worked 50 to 70 hours a week. Mothers stayed home to manage the household and tend to the children. Dad was very good at his trade and seemed always to have work. I can never recall being hungry because of either too little or poor quality of food.

My winter clothing was warm and always kept clean and in good repair by Mom. Almost every Saturday, I would have the ten cents needed to watch the triple feature of cowboy movies at the Center

Theater. Occasionally, Dad managed to treat us to a Sunday supper uptown at the Club Cafe.

During those Great Depression years, my employment consisted of collecting and selling scrap iron, brass, and copper that was found along the railways or abandoned mill yards, managing Kool-Aid stands, and selling magazines.

At nine or ten years of age, I was given the best gift of all. Uncle Sig, a successful Detroit engineer and tool steel company manager took me uptown to Kunze's Leather Goods store to buy me a bike. It was during the Great Depression and my parents could not squeeze out the money to buy one. It was a royal blue Schwinn with balloon tires, a handlebar basket, and mudguards.

I was soon to give my bike the true test of utility and endurance as I secured a paper carrier job for the Grand Rapids Press. A bike was essential to complete my route, which began downtown at the corner (alley level) of West Harris and Mitchell streets and ended on Sunnyside Drive (then named Popular Street) at the Pennsylvania Railroad tracks. The route, which included many side streets, was more than two miles long. It carried me through two treacherous winters on partially plowed roads and sub-zero temperatures to deliver my 40 daily papers for a weekly wage of $1.19. Dad's constant reminder sustained me: "If you live in Cadillac," he would say, "you must adjust to the cold, or expect to be miserable half of your life."

While I don't recall ever missing a delivery to a customer, I was sometimes "delayed" when invited to play a little football with the Lectkas, a very athletic family along my route. Never did I request nor was I ever given a ride in an automobile to carry out my delivery.

It was my responsibility to deliver the papers in a timely manner and I carried it out with nary a complaint from my customers. It was a major life lesson of discipline, responsibility, and organization that served me well throughout my life.

Almost every week, one dollar of my $1.19 earnings was invested in Defense Saving Stamps.

One time when my errant behavior brought Mom to quiet tears, my guilt feelings over the incident left me with some emotional turmoil. My remorse motivated me to visit the Johnson's Hardware store up on South Mitchell Street. I wanted to use my $1.19 weekly earnings for a gift for Mom. The clerk, obviously seeing a way to get a rather unattractive red donut shaped teapot removed from his inventory, recommended it as a nice gift for Mom. Upon receiving the gift, tears welled up in Mom's eyes once again, albeit tears of joy. That teapot now rests on a shelf in my current residence.

DEPRESSION ERA MEALS

Thou shouldst eat to live; not live to eat.
~ Socrates

I have never experienced sustained hunger. Well, once when I was about nine years old while camping with some friends in Brown's woods, some critters carried off our meat, bread, eggs, and sweets as we slept, forcing us to survive for two days on raw carrots dipped in peanut butter and mustard.

Every other day or so Mom would purchase a sack of groceries at the nearby Willis Market to supplement our stored food supplies. Grocery shopping during the 1930's was not complicated. One would tell the grocer what was wanted and wait for him to retrieve and put the items in a sack. If more than three or four items were to be purchased, the items would be written on paper by Mom and handed to the grocer.

I marveled at the quickness of the grocer's paper and string wrap of a slab of meat all the while keeping eye contact and conversation with the customer. No carts. No credit cards. No coupons. No 20 kinds of cereal from which to choose. No plastic bags. No electronic beeps at checkout. Just wait while the grocer retrieves your choices, wraps and puts them in paper sacks, adds up the bill while sometimes touching the lead pencil tip to his tongue to improve readability, and tells you what you owe. All financial transactions were by cash, check, or on tab.

Each morning, a man from a local dairy on his covered cart pulled by a horse, delivered milk to the front porch of our home. After the milk was consumed, the glass bottles would be washed and placed on the porch for retrieval by the deliveryman.

Ready-to-eat food packaging was in its infancy those days before World War II. Meals were typically prepared by creative housewives who kept their walk-in pantries and fruit cellars well stocked with the ingredients needed for well-balanced and tasty meals.

The fruit cellar in our home was an organizational masterpiece. It was accessed through a trap door in the woodshed immediately off the kitchen. Dad built shelves of every configuration needed to efficiently store the cans, jars, bags, and boxes of the mostly canned foods, which included a wide assortment of vegetables, meats, potatoes, apples, peaches, pears, cherries, plums, and wild fruits including raspberries, strawberries, blueberries, blackberries, and huckleberries.

Many fruits and vegetables were purchased or picked at harvest time from area farmers or the wood lots and stored temporarily for Mom's annual canning operation. The foods were cleaned and sliced or diced for canning, placed in jars, tagged with the dates and descriptions of contents, wax sealed, and stored in the fruit cellar's always-cool location.

Nearly all our food was harvested on farms and orchards within 50 miles of Cadillac. Workers from town often traded their services with area farmers for food. Dad might wallpaper or paint a McBain farmer's dining room for a few bushels of produce or a number of cleaned chickens to be dispensed to him over the following few months.

Our meals were healthy ones. The standard breakfast during winter was oatmeal, or its cousin, Ralston, a hot wheat cereal. I still remember words to the Ralston Company jingle. During warmer months, I would try to convince Mom to select boxed cereals based on the box top's value, which could be mailed in for toys and other prizes. Or, I might trade my box top with a collector friend.

Because I lived about four blocks from school, I returned home for lunch every day where I could expect hot soup, a pasta dish, or a sandwich. The evening meal would almost always include meat, mashed (or as I called them, "smashed,") potatoes, and a vegetable. I rejected spinach until I became a Popeye fan. Pancakes, usually the thin Swedish version, and waffles might be expected at any meal. Desserts were rare and between meal snacks would usually be a peanut butter sandwich and a glass of milk. The cookie jar was a kitchen counter mainstay.

During the 1930s and 1940s, obesity was uncommon. While the amount of food one consumed was probably not much different than today, the caloric content was somewhat less due primarily, I presume, to the absence of "junk" foods and much less sugar. Further, both young and old of those years were generally much more physically active. There being no television, pinball arcades, smart phones, or computer games, deserves much of the credit.

Housewives lacked the many labor saving devices found in kitchens today. During the 1930's, stove-heated water and iceboxes were being replaced with hot water heaters and refrigerators

    Might we conclude that increased physical activity combined with a more restrictive income (and considerably less sugar) will lead one to a healthier life? Probably.

*Author at 3 months
11830 Ward St. Detroit*

*Author at Cousin Bob's
Farm in Ludington*

*Author and Sig go hunting,
c. 1938*

Pat Chick in Lake City, c. 1931

MY CHILDHOOD CLOTHING

*Know, first, who you are
then adorn yourself accordingly.*
~ Epictetus

It is unlikely that those who create clothing fashions look to the 1930's for inspirations. It was a period of summer cottons and winter woolens, as the "miracle" fabrics appeared much later.

During the summer, we wore mostly long pants and short-sleeved shirts and undershirts. Dungarees, the precursor of jeans, were commonly seen especially when the play or work became physical. They were not acceptable for school, however. While shorts were seldom seen, many neighborhood boys spent most of their summer vacations in their swimming suits. With a Lake Cadillac swimming hole only two blocks from our house, less time was wasted changing clothes for a swim or two during the hot summer afternoons.

The ubiquitous "long-johns," those white undergarments with sleeves to the wrist and leg coverings to the ankle, were standard dress for boys during the coldest days of winter. They provided appropriate openings for nature's bodily functions and contained eight to ten buttons between the mid-section and the neck.

The layered look was the typical winter dress standard. A long sleeve wool shirt and a heavy wool sweater kept us warm in the sometime drafty homes and schoolrooms. For outdoor activities and the walks to school, we wore a mid-thigh-length overcoat, woolen mittens, and a hat with earflaps. One Christmas, Santa brought me an aircraft pilot's cap with goggles. I could not see well through the poor quality goggle lens, but I wore that cap with great pride and could not understand why Mom discouraged me from wearing it during the warm days of spring and fall.

Any discussion of 1930's clothing must include knickerbockers, or "knickers," those corduroy pants that provided cover from the waist to just below the knees, where they were kept in place by an elastic band. They were roomy and comfortable, but I never liked them, probably because my favorite foot-ware, high-tops, left a two or three - inch gap between the top of my boots and the knickers' elastic band.

There were basically four types of footwear for boys of the period; dress shoes, every day shoes, high-tops, and galoshes. Only dress shoes could be worn to Sunday school and a visit to Grandma's house.

The favored winter foot ware for boys were high-tops, which usually extended to the mid-calf or a little higher. They featured a special pocket for a jackknife, located on the outside of the right boot. A boy in those days would not be seen without his trusty jackknife! (Now aged 88, I continue to keep my jack knife with me at all times.) High-tops were not man's best invention, however. While they may keep snakes from biting you, they were impractical for winter wear in Northern Michigan. They had little insulation value and when they got wet from the snow or rain during the walk to school, discomfort set in which lasted throughout the school day. Some boys slipped their high-tops off which caused a rather unpleasant aroma around the schoolroom.

Play shoes were okay for school, but they must be cleaned and shined occasionally. The galoshes of those years were most always black with three or four buckles that provided for different levels of tightness. Many times, one or both of my galoshes mistakenly went home with a classmate and I went home with his. Not to worry! Tomorrow maybe the problem would be fixed although sometimes it would take several days. The first sign of the galoshes demise was a tear in the heel which could sometimes be corrected by an ample supply of electrical tape anchored by the skillful use of Mom's needle and strong thread. (I was often reminded to stop releasing my left galosh with the toes of my right shoe.)

We never complained, though. Dad frequently reminded me of his oft-repeated paraphrase of that ancient Persian saying; "I had the blues because I had no shoes until upon the street I met a man who had no feet." In September, 1942 I enrolled in Cadillac High School. I cast off the knickerbockers, high-tops, mittens, galoshes, and the pilot hat. Nice sweaters, windbreakers or lightweight jackets, ski caps, and gloves that were sometimes worn with hands in a fist to keep the fingers from freezing, I now had the proper teenage look.

Much to the annoyance of our parents, we liked to let shirttails hang out, roll our shirtsleeves to above the elbow, and roll our pants cuffs to the upper ankles to display our argyle-patterned socks. When in the presence of the other gender, caps were put away and we would not want to be seen wearing earmuffs.

During the war, the US government placed restrictions on the amount of material that could be used to produce a garment, so fashion designers had to be rather creative to maintain their livelihood. The T-shirt, introduced as an undergarment by the military during World War II, became a closet mainstay. Its cousin, the polo shirt, came later.

It was a good time to be a teenager. Almost anything you wore was acceptable because we all had to support the war effort.

My gold athletic letter sweaters, with their blue block "C," both in cardigan and pull-over styles, were usually worn on game Fridays and at many social and school functions.

MY TOY BOX

"Many inventions had their birth as toys"
~ Eric Hoffer

My toy box was located in a first-floor closet with a window. That little room on the sunny south side of our Wood Street (South Mitchell) home served as my comfort zone. Along with my toys, it contained most of my clothes and just about anything else that was my responsibility.

Much of my time, especially during seriously wet weather, was spent examining the various items in the box hoping to find some avenue to fun and adventure. In that three-foot square container, I might find a fire truck and some cars with missing wheels, and a large assortment of balls. The box held my shapeless ash gray baseball glove, handed down to me from Uncle Will, a member of Cadillac's well-respected travel team of the early 1900's.

In the box were several three-inch cubed blocks with numbers and letters on them, purchased many years earlier by Mom to prepare me for kindergarten. I would find the remains of a chemistry set that had kept me occupied for countless hours. There would be pieces of model airplanes made of fragile balsam wood smashed under pounds of toys. Scattered about were partial decks of cards and puzzle pieces, probably from several different scenes.

To defend our home against bad guys, I had a jack knife, toy pistols with Western-style holsters, a BB gun, and a few homemade slingshots. Because I played a rather good game of marbles, I had jars filled with my winnings

Near the bottom of the box rested several dozen three-to-four-inch-high lead soldiers, farmers, war materials, and animals, which could be manipulated to depict two scenes; soldiers at war and a bucolic farmyard. I spent hours plotting military attack and defense strategies making sure the American side won all battles. The enemy was made up of soldiers with chipped paint, a lost head, or some other disfigurement. I sometimes included cows and farmer Jacob in the battle scenes. When the weather permitted, I would take my farmers and soldiers outside to the sand box, where sticks, grass, pits from the plums that dropped from the tree, and other natural and manmade props added some realism to my fantasies.

    The literature in my toy box consisted of Little Big Books, which have been described as the size and shape of a four-inch square block sawed off the end of a two-by-four. Those books lead me through exciting adventure stories, usually about kids ridding their communities of evil and sinister men. Of course, there were many comic books featuring such champions of good as the Lone Ranger, Tarzan, Batman, Flash Gordon, Jack Armstrong, Buck Jones, Superman, Captain Marvel, and Tom Mix. Because children radio serials of the day featured many of those same heroes I may have assigned the wrong art form to a hero or two.

    During my early teens, I read some of the Jack London books and other outdoor adventure stories. "The Call of the Wild" and "White Fang" are remembered as among my favorite London stories.

    My toy box was also a hiding place for all sorts of things. I recall finding a single mitten. I probably lost its mate and thought that Mom might never know although she probably did, but wouldn't make an issue of the matter. There were a few first grade spelling and penmanship papers with far too many red marks on them to show Mom and Dad so into the toy box they went. In later years, I might have deposited a Valentine or two from some pretty classmates. I would not have wanted my parents or anyone to think that I would keep anything given to me by a girl! We wanted our friends to think that girls were our natural foes, although our "weapon" of choice was to ignore them rather than apply any form of unfriendliness or violence. That silly attitude changed sometime during my sixth and seventh grades.

As I entered my later years at Cooley Grade School, my toys were passed down to my brother Sig who was seven years younger than me. My Schwinn bicycle, my most prized possession, was a gift from my Uncle Sig when I was ten. It served me well when I delivered papers on my two-mile Grand Rapids Press route.

My interests turned to outdoor sports. I replaced my sled, kites, fire trucks, marbles, and lead soldiers with a good baseball glove, a regulation sized football, fishing tackle, upgraded skis, ice skates, a hockey stick, and a tennis racquet. Sports of all kinds became an important part of my life. My new venues included the Caberfae Ski Area and the Community Beach, both of which would later provide income for me.

Now as I approach the tenth decade of my life, my toys are few. I have returned to the bike, but do not use 4 of the 6 gears. My gearless bike of 77 years ago gave me the leg strength to enjoy a life filled with sports without any serious lower body injury and my current *Specialized* bike purchased from the local bike shop seems to be helping me similarly today. My golf clubs and tennis racquet have been collecting dust since my early 80's. My guns are gone, but the fishing pole is at the ready and is occasionally used.

My only other remaining toys are a pair of really good downhill skis and boots, which are upgraded frequently.

Boredom has never been among my problems.

PIANO LESSONS

"An intellectual is someone who can listen to the "William Tell Overture" without thinking of the Lone Ranger.
~ John Chesson

Mom was a very good pianist. She would play at family gatherings while we sang or hummed the tunes. During my childhood years, we always had a piano in our living room.

I was probably nine or ten years old during the Great Depression days when Mom and Dad decided that I should take piano lessons. My parents always seemed to agree on family matters. I was not happy with the thought of replacing my playground activities with moving my fingers over the black and whites.

Miss Dancer was a nice lady who lived a block from Cooley School. Once or twice a week after school I would spend about 30 minutes at her home working on the art. I recall that the lessons cost 50 cents per session so I took my practice seriously even though it was painful. Of course, Miss Dancer, to keep her pupil, told Mom, "Toppie has a lot of potential and should continue."

After a few weeks Mom had me continue lessons with Mrs. Colby who lived up near Diggins Hill on Holbrook Street. She soon noted that "Toppie" lost interest in Piano and mercifully released me from my agony.

NEIGHBORHOOD CLUBS

Seize the day.
Make your lives extraordinary.
~ Dead Poets Society

We formed clubs frequently, but they seldom lasted more than one or two days. Democracy was alive and well on Wood Street. It just couldn't be sustained. The upside was that we all had many chances to be "leaders." If my friends didn't choose me, I could simply form my own club and install myself as president, or general, or some such title. The clubs seldom had a purpose. After election of the officers, a meeting site had to be created. Members gathered tarps, old stools, rope, boxes, boards, rugs, and other items from their parent's garages, which were then carted to the "office" site, typically under a large tree on a vacant lot.

The first order of "business" was to select a name and representative colors for our club. Many names were taken from athletic teams such as Tigers, Wildcats, Wolverines, Spartans, Bears, and, of course, Vikings. Wimpy names, such as Cubs, Orioles, Browns, Red Sox, Buckeyes, and Gophers were never considered.

At our new "office," we sat and talked about sports, people, cowboy movies, and the new family on the block. That evening, or the following day, the club was dissolved and the building materials were returned to their rightful places.

BOY SCOUTS

Scouting reinforced values we brought from home. It gave us an opportunity to share them with others whose values were not as strong.
~ Jose Nino

At age 12, I joined the Boy Scouts of America, Cooley School Troop #28. Scouting was a significant experience for me as I learned lifelong social and leadership skills. I also learned to avoid eating unwashed cherries that have been sprayed with insect repellant.

The nation was at war and manpower was in short supply. The scouts of Troop #28 were called on to camp at a cherry orchard near Traverse City and assist with the harvest. Those juicy morsels, dangling from the trees and white with bug spray, offered a temptation that I was unable to resist! My parents had to retrieve their very sick son from the farm before my full contribution to the harvesting effort was completed.

We learned woodland skills in the Cooley School gymnasium. On Saturdays, we would take day trips to nearby Brown's Woods to practice what we learned. Trudging through the snow and accompanied by the Scout Master and a maybe a father or two, we sought a small clearing where we set up the day's learning laboratory. There we practiced fire building, cooking, and survival skills. Time was spent observing and identifying animal tracks and birds.

About once a year, the entire troop would attend the Scenic Trails Honors Council meetings and Camping Jubilees where we met with Boy Scouts from other communities. I remember those held in forested areas near Manistee and Traverse City. It was a thrill to be called to the front of the group and be presented with merit badges and other achievement awards at an assembly attended by hundreds of scouts and their parents.

As a Boy Scout, however, I was a mild failure. I earned over 20 merit badges and attained Star and Life Scout levels, but fell just short of the awards needed to be an Eagle Scout.

When I was the admissions director at the University of Michigan I was interviewed by a Readers' Digest writer for about 30 minutes. At one point, I proclaimed that we looked for leadership qualities of applicants and that achieving Eagle Scout recognition spoke volumes about the candidate's character and determination. In her very short paragraph from that telephone interview, the reporter wrote in the July 1988 edition, published in about 30 languages for world circulation, that I had failed to achieve that lofty distinction of Eagle Scout!

CADILLAC SCHOOL CAMP (TORENTA)

Camp Doxie was organized in 1906 on a four and one half acre plot at the entrance to Big Cove on Lake Mitchell. During the following 32 years, the site served the children of the Cadillac area as a YMCA camp with four cabins, a lodge, and a small director's cabin.

Financial difficulties in 1938 led to the sale of the camp. The "Y" priced the facility at $10,000 but would sell it to a local buyer for $3,000, presumably with the understanding that it would continue as a children's camp. Two leading educators, both YMCA members, B. C. Shankland, Cadillac's superintendent of schools, and legendary Cass School principal, Lynn Corwin, convinced the school board to purchase the camp. It became one of first school-owned camps in the US.

Corwin became the first director and his wife, Marie, the camp Mother. They held those positions until

1957. In 1942 the camp was expanded to about 170 acres. In 1953 the name was changed to Camp Torenta, an Indian term for "land of the tall pines.

My first experience at the Cadillac School Camp began June 28, 1939, the first week of the first year the new camp operated. The weekly fee was $5. Each of the four cabins could accommodate eight campers.

As a shy, skinny ten-year-old kid, I recall the anxiety of waiting for the bus to arrive at Cooley School to transport us to camp. It was my first experience away from my family. I was fearful.

Mom had packed my essentials for the weeklong experience. Included were bedding, changes of clothes, swimming suit, jack knife, pre-addressed stamped post cards to be sent home, soap and towel, too many sweaters, a book, tooth brush and paste, softball glove, an extra pair of shoes, and money for snacks and crafts. From Cooley School, the bus stopped at two or three other elementary schools before making its way to the Big Cove camp.

Lynn Corwin soon put most of my fears at ease with his warm greetings. We departed the bus and were directed to our cabins where I claimed an upper bunk in cabin Number One. From dawn to dusk (and later,) Cadillac School Camp offered a non-stop menu of activities. My favorites were softball, swimming, canoeing, hiking, and evening campfires.

Because I had spent many hours in the Lake Cadillac swimming hole near my home, I was among the first to qualify for access to the diving platform in deep water. It was a good confidence builder for me.

The only craft that interested me was weaving whistle lanyards. I returned home with about three multi-colored lanyards for each whistle I owned. The week included a surprise birthday party for me at the Monday evening meal. To this day, I don't know how they knew it was my birthday.

While many friendships were created, I soon learned that not all boys played fair and a few were true bullies. "Fred," (pseudonym to protect the innocent) remembered by some of my friends even today as one of the meanest kids in town, was assigned to my cabin. We were all afraid of Fred. I supposed I would greet my parents at week's end with fewer teeth and maybe one or two darkened eyes. But for some reason Fred took a liking to me. With him as my pal, I had no problems with the camp's lesser bullies. By week's end I felt somewhat comfortable around those few mischievous campers primarily because I got to know them rather well. They seemed to adapt gradually as they began to relish the camping experience. Understanding human behavior was nicely facilitated in Lynn Corwin's camp.

As I look back on that camp experience I feel that it helped me understand why and how people behave the way they do. Fred unintentionally taught me that if I work at it there would be no reason to dislike anybody. I met and forged friendships with boys from different parts of town, some rich, others poor, a few from the Catholic school, and even one or two from out of town. While I could not understand the psychological forces at work, I began to realize that there were good and interesting people from places other than Cooley School. It helped me to appreciate and enjoy other people and subsequently otherworld cultures. At week's end, I even considered Fred as my friend.

I regret that our community has not maintained that living and learning experience for today's 10 to 13 year olds. Maybe young people today would benefit greatly in a camp setting where they would learn important social behaviors without electronic devices and other manufactured amusements. My experience at camp had a significant positive impact on my life.

From its beginning, the camp has been substantially supported by service clubs and many other groups and individuals by making sure that all children regardless of their ability to pay the fees could enjoy the camping experience. Community groups also subsidized land improvements and structural expansions. I remain proud of Cadillac and its citizens.

At that time, I could not imagine that one day far into the future (1957) I would become the camp's second director. During my brief tenure, I researched and assigned Native American tribal names to the cabins. (After two years, I resigned my camp position to accept a generous financial package to attend the University of Michigan School of Graduate Studies.)

A SWEDISH CHRISTMAS CELEBRATION

Christmas waves a magic wand over this world, and behold, everything is softer and more beautiful.
~ Norman Vincent Peale

Christmas was a very special time of the year for the Sjogrens. All relatives on Dad's side of the family lived in Michigan, concentrated in the Detroit area, Ludington, and Cadillac. All 25 or 30 of us convened for the festivities each year in Cadillac.

The Swedish Christmas Eve dinner and gift exchange took place at our Wood Street home. Several days before the guests arrived, Mom began the preparation of the Christmas Eve dinner while Dad made gallons of *drika* (root beer) timing the production so that it would be tasteful but not too strong at Christmastime.

Our Swedish dinner was a taste delight! Derived from "peasant" foods of 19th Century Sweden, traditional Christmas dining consisted of *korv* (potato sausage,) *sillsallat* (a cold meat dish,) *sylta* (jellied veal,) meatballs, herring, *dopp I grytan*, (bread dipped in gravy,) lingonberry preserves, *limpa* (light rye bread,) all of which was anchored by the infamous *lutefisk*e.

Lutefisk has been described as a, "... *Scandinavian specialty made with unsalted dried codfish. The age-old preparation method is to soak the dried cod in regularly changed cold water for a period of eight days. The cod is then soaked for two days in a mixture of potash lye and water, after which it is soaked for two more days in fresh water.) The final step is simmering the fish for 10 to 15 minutes, until it becomes translucent. Just before serving, the lutefisk is sprinkled with allspice, salt, and white pepper. It's accompanied with white sauce and boiled potatoes."* (From The Food Lover's Companion, 2nd edition, by Sharon Tyler Herbst.) Today, fans of this dish enjoy ready-to-cook lutefisk that is commercially available.

Desserts included pies, rice pudding and the ever-present *pepparkakor* (thin spice cookies colored and shaped in Christmas themes.) For house guests the following morning breakfast fare would be stacks of thin and tasty Swedish pancakes, sausage, and boiled coffee brewed with egg whites mixed in the grounds.

As elsewhere, our Christmas on Wood Street was for children. After dinner on Christmas Eve while the dishes were being washed, someone would take the youngest children upstairs to the bedroom window to watch for Santa Clause. The jolly old man was a clever one, though. I never saw him arrive, but when we returned to the living room, the tree was magically surrounded by stacks of brightly colored packages. All the relatives had gathered in the living room for the opening of the gifts.

Following the gift exchange and a few piano carols by Mom, the adults and older children celebrated *Julafton* (Christmas Eve) services at the Zion Lutheran Church on East Nelson Street at 11:00 PM.

On Christmas Day, Grandma and Grandpa Sjogren hosted the family for a sumptuous Christmas Day (*Juldag*) dinner at their home at 216 East Nelson Street, near their church. When aging took its toll on Grandma, Uncle George and Aunt Franie Currier hosted the family for Christmas dinner at their nearby home at 212 East Nelson Street.

The Christmas season in Cadillac was an absolutely splendid occasion for all.

THE WOODS

Let us permit nature to have her way. She understands her business better than we do.
~ Michel de Montaigne

The great forests that surrounded Cadillac influenced much of my early life. Even though Dad worked long hours as a house painter and decorator, he would pitch a tent for the family at a nearby lake where we would hike, swim, fish, and observe nature. We enjoyed perch, bass, or walleye over a kerosene stove or campfire. Mom was an excellent outdoor cook and she loved the woods.

I often ventured into the woods near our home alone or maybe with a friend to closely examine the magic of the forest. I would roll over a rotting log separating it from its long-held position and, on my knees, observe the ecological wonders that came alive in the dampened soil. Crawling bugs and worms would scurry for cover as the sudden turmoil upset their quiet existence. When I returned to my destructive scene after a few minutes, I would see the delicate footprints of songbirds that had dropped in for a snack. Understandably, the squirrels and birds of the forest will be more wary of people than their urban cousins, but their chirping and peeping let me know that I was in their territory.

While few people took vacations during the 1930s, our family enjoyed a camping experience nearly every summer. Munising in the Upper Peninsula was a favorite vacation destination where I was convinced that my early June swimming in Lake Superior defined me as a true child of the North, albeit one who experienced cold induced numbness and blue skin from the frigid waters!

Our entire family, along with Aunt Pearl and Uncle Will, accompanied by his dog, Duke, would often hunt, fish, pick up pine knots for firewood, pick arbutus for display in our home (it was acceptable then,) and harvest wild strawberries, raspberries, and huckleberries. Many delightful hours were spent in the woods with Dad and Uncle Will explaining nature's work to me, while the ladies cooked a tasty meal on the small portable gas stove.

With my heavy job-related travel, I used my vacation time for family activities. A pop-up camper towed by a sedan or station wagon, took us to camping sites from the West Coast to the East Coast including a New Jersey site where we enjoyed the campfire while observing a strolling deer and the night lights of Manhattan across the Hudson River.

FAMILY AUTOMOBILES

When preparing to travel, lay out all your clothes and all your money. Then take half the clothes and twice the money.
~ Susan Heller

I recall with nostalgia our family's 1928 Ford Model A Coupe. The four of us would slide into the only seat; Dad the driver, me in the middle with one leg on each side of the floor-mounted stick shift, and Mom at the passenger door with my brother Sig on her lap.

My tolerance for cold weather was probably the result of spending many hours in that car with its side curtains and a barely functioning heater.

We parked downtown during summer evenings where we watched and conversed with strolling citizens. Sometimes on rural roads, I convinced Dad to let me sit in the opened trunk with my feet dangling over the rear bumper. It would be allowed only when there was little traffic and Mom was willing to sit twisted in her seat to watch in case I fell to the roadway.

A 1928 Ford Model A Coupe

One cold January day when I was about five years old, Grandpa Sjogren, Dad, and I were returning from a relative's farm near Ludington with a partially butchered pig. We became trapped by a fierce winter storm near Leroy. In those days, snowplows were not able to hoist snow over the high banks. As the storm gained intensity, the driving areas narrowed until there was only a lane the width of the snowplow. When the plow had no place to deposit the snow, the road was closed, sometimes for several days.

Luckily, a friendly farmer appeared at our car and invited us to his home for food and a bed for that night. Dad cut off a chunk of pork for the family as gratitude for their kindness. It was during the Great Depression and strangers helped each other

In 1941, Dad purchased a new green four-door Chevrolet. It was one of the last cars made before the outbreak of World War II. (Coincidently, I now drive a green four-door Chevrolet!) The automobile manufacturers re-tooled their factories to build tanks, trucks, airplanes, and other war materials needed to defeat our enemies.

The car lacked many of the features on today's vehicles. Because it had a clutch to shift gears, the driver had to coordinate the timing between the release and engagement of the clutch pedal and the accelerator, often resulting in jerky starts. There were no seat belts, radios, shatterproof windshields, back-up lights, steel-belted tires, window washers, or turn signals. To turn left, the driver rolled down the manually operated window and extended his arm at 180 degrees. A right turn required a 90-degree angle with the left lower arm extended skyward.

The headlight dimmer switch was located on the floor where it was activated by the driver's left foot. All seating was on bench seats that, while less comfortable than the buckets on today's autos, worked very well when one was on a date. I learned how to steer with one hand using a "suicide" spinner knob installed on the steering wheel. Parents taught their teenagers how to drive, change tires, and check the water and oil levels.

Because pleasure driving was discouraged during the war, a gas-rationing plan was implemented. Most families were issued "A" stickers, which allowed about three gallons of gas per week. Health workers, ministers, and those who used their cars for essential safety and war-related activities were issued "B" or "C" stickers, which allowed extra gas. Drivers were urged to drive under the "Victory Speed" of 35 miles per hour. Few families had a second car.

The severe gas restrictions were imposed primarily to conserve rubber. The US had adequate supplies of oil, but most rubber was imported from the Dutch East Indies (now Indonesia) and tires usually lasted no more than two or three years. Without vast supplies of rubber the wartime manufacturing efforts would take a serious blow.

Most people accepted the restrictions on their gas usage as well as rationed meats, sugar, and coffee. Cigarettes and alcohol were in short supply.

It was wartime and we were expected to make sacrifices! One did not worry much about the authorities if rationing standards were violated. Your fellow citizens would consider you unpatriotic and not supportive of the war effort, a far worse punishment at that time. Few would brag about their successes in securing an extra bag of sugar or five gallons of gas without ration stamps.

Dad bought a used pick-up truck on which he built a wooden enclosure over the cargo bed to keep his supplies secure and out of the weather. At times, he allowed me to remove the enclosure and cart a group of friends to the Pine or Clam River, or other spots where we would enjoy time together. Footballs were tossed about to impress the girls, campfires were built to roast hot dogs and marshmallows, and usually some off-key singing ensued. For overnight camping trips, the enclosure was most welcomed on the truck.

Smoking, drugs, and drinking adult beverages were considered unacceptable teen-age behaviors and were seldom practiced. Such vices were generally not a part of the early 1940's teenage culture.

With our limited gas allotment, we could occasionally motor around lakes Cadillac and Mitchell, drive to fishing and hunting sites, picnic in the woods, and occasionally have enough fuel to drive our dates to the dance or a movie house.

It was yet another advantage of living in Cadillac. Most of life's necessities and pleasures were close at hand!

Sketch of 1932 Plymouth four-door sedan comparable to one owned by Pat and the author in 1955.

GROWING UP DURING A TROUBLED TIME

Adolescence is a period of rapid changes. Between the ages of 12 and 17, for example, a parent ages as much as 20 years
- Unknown

We often hear about the numerous difficulties one faced growing up through the Great Depression and the World War II eras. During the 1930's most families were struggling to meet their financial responsibilities. Later, our lives were consumed by the many sacrifices we had to make to support the war effort. Those two worldwide forces, the economy and the war, most likely helped to ameliorate some traditionally challenging conditions both parents and teachers had to contend with, namely, childhood behaviors and discipline.

Some might say that we were too poor to be "bad boys." If you tossed a stone through a neighbor's window, you or your parents had to pay for it. We avoided destructive behaviors. Seldom were both parents employed during the depression years, so moms remained home to watch over the children's activities.

We took our responsibilities for the care and protection of our toys and clothing seriously, as there was seldom money for replacement should they be lost or destroyed. And, of course, there were far fewer child psychologists in those days who insisted that parents allow their children to display their bad behaviors in any way they wished lest they grow up to be neurotic "basket cases."

During the war years, gas rationing gave parents an excuse to deny their older children use of the family sedan. Much teenage socially explosive steam was released by walking across town to pick up your date, return downtown to the movie house, accompany her home, and trek back to your home. Car use today gives teenagers an exposure to many of life's temptations that are unavailable to walkers. Because we came of driving age during the fuel restrictive 1940's, we didn't miss the car culture that became so prevalent for later generations.

As I look back on my childhood, I have concluded that my parents were very good disciplinarians. I don't recall ever being spanked, grounded for days, or sent to bed without supper. I was never called a "bad boy" nor did Mom or Dad ever say that they were dissatisfied with my general behavior. It must have been difficult for them to repress their feelings at those times that I did disappoint them. When I exhibited bad behavior, which probably happened more than occasionally, Dad would simply tell me what I did was wrong and make me promise that in the future I would think before acting.

Occasionally I would be sent to my room for a short while to contemplate my behavior. While I don't think he ever voiced such, I always felt that his expectations of me were very high which seemed to motivate me to accept his guidance and continually strive to achieve those lofty goals of good behavior. I grew up with a dogmatic determination to not disappoint my parents in any way.

Mom, always the quiet supporter of Dad's child rearing methods, worried when I failed to appear home at an expected time. I once told her that I was late getting home from school because I took a shortcut. It was true! A straight line from Cooley School to our home on Wood Street took me through a small wetland area that had all kinds of things to interest young boys. There I would enjoy the always standing water (or ice), frogs, snakes, bugs, and an abandoned well. That well proved to be a center of adventure, one that could be entered and exited with a bit of courage and athleticism, albeit a pastime that surely would be seen today as dangerous and maybe illegal.

After that episode, whenever I was late for a meal or an event, I would be asked, "Did you find another shortcut home?"

Maybe growing up during the Great Depression helped us to adjust to adverse social and economic conditions in later years. Because we did not experience the more affluent and carefree life of the Roaring Twenties, we did not know that we were living under economic hardships. I have since observed during many experiences in Third and Fourth World countries that people of those places seem to be happy and possess similar hopes and expectations for a better future for their children just as we did.

As I grew older, my parents often reminded me of the difficulties they faced during the 1930's. How difficult it must have been to raise a family with so few resources and the constant lingering anxieties of unemployment.

Taking responsibility for my behavior served me well during my teenage years of the 1940's. While some of my friends were required to be home at a certain time, I seldom had such restrictions placed on me. It strengthened my confidence when my parents suggested, not mandated, that if I was not home at the usual time I should call and advise them of my whereabouts. During my later teenage years the calls were less necessary. I liked to think that it was because they trusted me, although it was probably because they did not want to be awakened during those late hours.

Boys will be boys and I'm sure that I brought consternation to my parents on many occasions that passed without punishment or even discussion. Mom and Dad may have rightly assumed that disciplined behavior that was learned and applied in school would have beneficial carry over effects at home.

What I did learn from my parents that has since been applied successfully to our four children, is that if youngsters are treated as mature, intelligent people capable of being responsible decision-makers they will usually assume adulthood as mature, intelligent people capable of making responsible decisions. It worked for me and I suspect that it would work well for most people.

COOLEY GRADE SCHOOL

It is the mark of an educated mind to be able to entertain a thought without accepting it.
~ Aristotle

In September 1933, I entered kindergarten at Cooley Grade School on Granite Street, about four blocks from our Wood Street home. My feet and later my blue Schwinn bicycle were my only forms of transport to and from school.

Elementary school was generally easy for me. While I was an average student as defined by grades, I may have been an above average "learner" as my experiences there were positive and prepared me well for more serious study and work experiences in future years.

Report cards in those days included grades earned as well as statements about the student's behavior, health, schoolwork habits, and social adjustments. Even today those evaluations provide me with some pleasant as well as a few not so pleasant memories of my early years. I knew how to reach the teacher's minimum expectations and I had almost no parental pressure to earn better grades, although my parents expected me to take my learning seriously.

My school reports show that I was usually above average in social skills, arithmetic, reading, and social studies, but I was poor in penmanship and a "disturbance" in music. Comments from those grade school reports included "not working to his ability, enjoying fun, but not in a smarty way, shy, is kind and plays fair, a leader, good thinker, bad speller, and works a bit too fast." My fourth grade teacher penned, "He seems to show a great interest in geography and history." (Perceptive words, indeed!) I enjoyed school and I liked my teachers.

My elementary education was memorable in a most literal sense. I still remember the names of all my grade school teachers: Miss "Winnie" Rice, kindergarten, and grades one through eight respectively were Miss Henderson, Miss Thompson, Miss Lockwood, Miss VanderWal, Miss Peterson, Miss Lindell, Mr. Brown, and Miss Levine.

All of them were unwed, although Miss Thompson and Mr. Brown were married after I left for high school. They were all good teachers, albeit rather strict, who carried out their duties in classrooms that lacked the frills found in today's learning centers.

The school day began with the Pledge of Allegiance to the American flag. We sat in efficiently aligned writing desks. Pictures of presidents Washington and Lincoln and a world map graced each classroom. The windows rattled in response to the cold north winds of Cadillac.

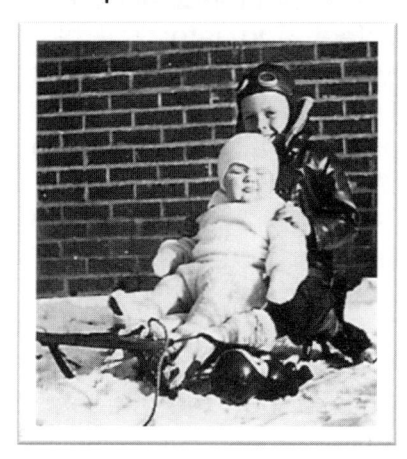

Author and Sig on sled

The teachers most certainly did not subscribe to my parents' liberal discipline strategies. They were demanding and didn't smile often. Classroom instruction was formal and one did not speak unless called upon. Cut-ups in class might be sent to the cloakroom or get slapped on the wrist by the teacher's ruler. I got one of those ruler treatments in the third grade for teasing the girl who sat in front of me.

Soccer, marbles, or softball was usually played during recess on the sand, snow, or mud covered playground behind the school. A circular climbing bar apparatus, seesaws, and swings were also available. Cooley School had a gymnasium where the main activities were dodge ball, foot races, and basketball. Boys and girls were separated for all games and contests.

Most classes consisted of lectures, reading, arithmetic, social and natural sciences, cursive writing, and spelling drills, each of which was followed by the teacher directing questions mostly toward underachieving students. We read classical and some popular literature of the period. As historical events were studied, noteworthy people and dates were put to memory, as quizzes were frequent. Few textbooks were ever removed from the school. The classroom teachers were also responsible for art and music instruction.

The teacher would write the homework assignment on the blackboard for all to copy. Time would be allowed during the school day and I was usually able to complete the assignment during that time. Lengthy reports occasionally required visits to the public library on weekends.

Because I valued my playtime, my schoolwork could probably be best defined as quickly done, but rarely well done.

For most of my research and writing assignments, I relied on a family gift from Uncle Sig; a new complete set of *Encyclopedia Britannica*, a works of some 16 or 18 volumes consisting of large pages, small print and few photographs. Those magical books are still regarded as the most scholarly of all encyclopedias. An American once invested roughly three hours per night for four and a half years to read the entire 11th edition of the *Encyclopedia Britannica*. It proved to be a valuable learning tool throughout my pre-university education. When boredom set in, I would sometimes browse a volume to read items that sparked my interest.

Sports were a major interest for me at Cooley. During the 1930s, there were no community-organized sports; thus, our only serious sports competition took place between the six elementary schools during the school year. Soccer was my favorite sport although I played basketball, touch football, and softball as well.

We walked to all schools to compete, a somewhat challenging task during the winter. We especially looked forward to away games at Cass and Whittier grade schools on the north side of town as we could take the direct route across the eastern end of Lake Cadillac. Of course, we were advised by teachers to keep our distance from the open waters at the Clam River and ice harvesting operations.

There were no school buses or lunchrooms. Because I returned home for lunch, I had busy highway crossings (US-131 and M-55,) eight times each day, or some number over 10,000 times during my nine years at Cooley. During my last two years at Cooley School I was a school crossing guard on the corner of Wood and Granite streets.

SPORTS AND GAMES

*We could never have loved the earth
so well if we had no childhood in it.*
~ George Eliot

As a child, I became addicted to nearly all sports and games. First, it was Cooley Grade School and sandlot team sports, followed by varsity sports in high school and college, and continuing on with both team and individual sports well into my later years.

My love affair with sports began rather early in my life. On my three-block trek to Cooley School from my home I would dribble soccer-style a small can to school. It was hard on my shoes during those Great Depression years and maybe a bit dangerous because of the two major highways that had to be crossed, but the satisfaction of achieving my goal was worth the slight risk involved. I would sometimes hide my battered can at school for the return trip home.

Many of my sporting adventures took advantage of the hills, forests, waters, and good snows and ice of the Cadillac area. Thanks to my grandparents for their wise decisions to settle in this remarkable environment.

Alpine skiing has always been my favorite sport. Although I have skied the hills and mountains for more than 80 years, I now ski the "blues" rather than the more challenging, "blacks." So far, I have conquered the slopes at three-dozen ski resorts located among six states and five foreign countries. *(See chapter on Alpine Skiing.)*

Organized softball was first played at age eleven at Cooley School followed by the Cadillac city leagues, college fraternity, US Navy, U of M staff team, and finally at the University of Southern California at age 63. At the U of M, I was the third baseman with the Ann Arbor Turkeys, a travel team that "gobbled" up few opponents. Interesting team names in Ann Arbor! While I was a Turkey, my son, Sig, was quarterback for the Ann Arbor Huron High School River Rats football, baseball, and hockey teams.

As a pre-teen, my neighborhood contests included football (sans pads,) boxing, soccer, softball, tag, and hide-and-seek. Besides softball at Cooley School it was the playground apparatus, dodge ball, basketball, marbles, and soccer.

Ice-skating and hockey at the Diggins Park rink and occasionally on the lake two blocks from my home helped make the winter season pass quickly. Cross-country skiing and snowshoeing were enjoyed a few times.

I relished snowball fights, ice fishing, and canoe trips on the Pine River.

During the 1930's the City blocked off north and south bound Oak and South Simons streets at Stimson Street for a few hours for late afternoon and early evening sledding. North side kids had a similar arrangement at either North or Bremer Street. During those Depression years, most of us had hand-me-down sleds. The ones with the longest sleds were envied because they were considerably faster. With the street's hard surface beneath us, we often returned home with damaged trousers and jackets giving evidence that we used elbows and knees to maneuver through the throngs of fellow sled riders and walkers returning to the launch point at the top of the hill.

During my teens and later I was on the varsity football, basketball, and track teams at CHS. My most significant sport recognitions were running the 880-yard dash at CHS and Central Michigan, although track was an activity of little interest to me.

I played tennis and baseball. Waterskiing, swimming, pool, sailing, and ping-pong were enjoyed, well into my adult years. I have tossed horseshoes and Frisbees, batted badminton birds, released arrows from my trusty bow, stroked croquet balls, bowled, and sailed a canoe on small lakes. Table and deck shuffleboard, volleyball, squash, racquetball, pickleball, bocce ball, and handball were all experienced.

My parents introduced me to fishing before I entered kindergarten. Walleye, bass, and stream fishing for trout were favorites. Once in a two-man rubber raft in some shallow Atlantic waters near Key West, I hooked a small hammerhead shark. In an instant, he swam away with my bait, as well as my pole and reel, which wisely were quickly released!

Both deer and small game hunting led me to the woods during Michigan's colorful fall seasons. During the 1950's, I harvested three bucks. Shooting rats at the city dump behind the cemetery with a 22-caliber rifle was fun. (I suppose today, a young lad walking through the neighborhood with a 22-rifle would generate some 911 calls.)

I have both snorkeled and scuba dived in the Pacific Ocean. Golf was on my recreational agenda mostly for the camaraderie with friends and family. There have been countless hours spent on family carrom boards, bean-bag, and dart games.

Team sports in the neighborhood church lot consumed many hours during my elementary school years. Youngsters learned life's lessons in those venues. Because there were no organized sports competitions other than a few sponsored by the schools, we organized our own games and rules for fair play. The life lessons learned because of our playground culture remain with me today. (And when a misdirected ball landed in Mrs. Donahue's flowerbed, I learned how to ask forgiveness!)

While I enjoy the competition, I do not feel that I am overly competitive. I possessed average athletic ability, with above average skills in Alpine skiing, racquetball, and tennis and below average abilities in basketball and golf.

Contrary to some current featured "sports" on ESPN, I do not consider NASCAR, poker, and swimsuit competitions worthy of the "sport" designation. (I was rather good at poker, but would have failed miserably in the other two!)

In 1960, because of my job-related travel, I gave up most time-consuming sports away from family for those that could be spent with my wife and children. We enjoyed travel, camping, fishing, and cycling along with a lot of downhill skiing that included many trips to the Colorado resorts during spring vacations.

(Note: Please see Appendix Seven for a complete list sports, games, and the arts.)

SPORT VENUES: THEN AND NOW

*Individual commitment to a group effort —
that is what makes a team work, a company work, a
society work, a civilization work.*
~ Vince Lombardi

One redeeming feature of a memoir is to compare current ways of doing things with one's past experiences in similar activities. The organization and conduct of schoolboy sports have changed dramatically during the past 60 years.

My grandson, Wes, who lives in a Detroit suburb, is an excellent hockey player. His teams played before large crowds on rinks throughout Michigan, including the Joe Lewis Arena in Detroit. His 40-game season, under the direction of three coaches, lasted from October to April. The team's web page listed his achievements: Captain, leading scorer, and the "most valuable player" award. His team was provided with colorful, professional-looking uniforms and the best equipment. A Zamboni refreshed the ice between periods.

Wes was nine years old at that time!

While today's pre-teens benefit by the many and varied sports activities that are generally well managed by dedicated men and women, something may be missing. Are we denying today's children the opportunity to learn life's lessons by over supervising, over spending, and over programming their out-of-school activities?

Children these days spend their earlier years on carefully crafted playgrounds with their spiffy uniforms and well-designed equipment, at contests organized and supervised by adults, and under the critical eyes of their cheering and sometimes complaining parents.

The thrills of receiving trophies, publicity, team travel, team uniforms, and other experiences, once delayed until high school years and beyond, are now in danger of being "used up" before the child has attained the maturity to make wise decisions about his or her teenage thrill seeking activities. Unfortunately, some will later seek their "thrills" by engaging in self-destructing behaviors. It causes one to wonder if today's political and business leaders would demonstrate a bit more civility, creativity, and responsibility in the conduct of their work and politics if they had been afforded the opportunity of completely adult-free playground experiences with all of its intrinsic features.

I often reminisce about my early years in Cadillac. During the 1930s and early 1940s, most fathers who had jobs worked six days a week while mothers managed their labor-intensive homes, leaving them and their neighbors little time to become involved in their children's playtime.

Children of the 1930's amused themselves by organizing and playing pick-up sports and games of all kinds. Tackle football sans pads or headgear, boxing, softball, ice and street hockey, and soccer were played on vacant lots, churchyards, school playgrounds, and in open fields. At that time, there were no adult organized sport programs for young children other than those sponsored by Cadillac's six elementary schools. In sandlot sports it was up to the participants to agree on the rules and to conduct their own officiating. It worked that way because cheating would quickly lead to the end of the contest.

Many life lessons were practiced and learned during those games, including leadership, team play, good sportsmanship, cooperation, loyalty, and acceptable winning and losing behaviors. When teams were formed, the younger, smaller, or less athletically endowed boy would be the last chosen, but the contestants on both sides would usually "cut him some slack" so he could enjoy the experience.

It takes real-life experience to be a good leader and a good follower and we should not deny our young citizens those experiences. My generation learned fair play, honesty, team work, even a workable political process, as well as good competition with friendly adversaries. We learned ways of choosing leaders and devised clever strategies to keep neighborhood bullies from dominating the activities. We were living evidence that children are fully capable of learning life's lessons without the constant presence of adults.

As I approach the later years of my life, I reflect often on the lessons I learned growing up in Cadillac. One might wonder if today's children with their many highly programmed and adult managed activities are similarly advantaged. I think not!

During the summer, we hiked to Bells and Browns woods and visited the sandpits and swamps to find snakes, turtles, and frogs. We would capture them, keep them for a while primarily to learn what they would eat, and then release them. Mom said if I took care of them, I could bring home a few turtles and frogs, which I did, but the snakes were to remain in their natural habitats. We usually became quite attached to our new - found pets and never harmed the creatures. It was always a "catch and release" process.

While I enjoyed a few indoor activities such as stamp collecting, reading, cards, board games, teasing my little brother, and radio programs, I was from early on an outdoor child. Friendly snowball fights with the neighborhood kids became a passion. We built elaborate snow forts decorated with homemade flags.

Through the long Cadillac winters, I kept myself occupied by sledding, skating, and skiing. Frequently, I made the two-mile trek to Diggins Hill, the lighted city skating and hockey rinks where I had some of my most memorable experiences. While melodic skating music was playing, we enjoyed the ice and the hot chocolate in the wood heated railway boxcar that served as a warming hut.

We sometimes watched Cadillac's highly competitive hockey team usually defeat their rivals from the bigger cities of southern Michigan. I played the game often and developed a rather good shot. By time I was of age to compete, the war was in progress and the community's priorities were directed to more important activities.

Because of the shortened number of daylight hours, skiing was mostly a weekend activity. I cannot recall my first experience on skis, as I was very young when I first inserted my galoshes into the straps of my three-foot maples.

Our favorite slopes were in the Maple Hill cemetery area. There we worked on our ski technique in the Devil's Kettle and among the tombstones, which proved to be unforgiving slalom gates. Devil's Kettle, the site of Memorial Day services at that time, was a steep and heavily wooded terrain. We would point our three-or four-foot maple skis with toe straps toward what appeared to be a navigable line between the trees to the bottom. When a sudden surge of bravado or perhaps stupidity captured our interest, we would schuss the tree-filled bowl.

Many a skier hobbled home with a sore body part or two and with blood and tears merging to create rather colorful patterns on their faces. We might even cross-country to the nearby gravel pits to test those 45-degree slopes. Somehow we survived those many incursions into danger. It's a small wonder that we did not become permanent residents of one of Michigan's most beautiful cemeteries!

Playing on frozen Lake Cadillac was another pastime of the era. One day I had to apply my life saving skills by pulling from the icy waters my friend, Bruce, who had broken through the ice near the Peterson-Westberg block-ice storage facility. Fortunately, with a long two-by-four from a nearby sawmill, I was able to get him and his very heavy water-soaked woolens home before hyperthermia set in. While Dad was pleased with my life saving deed, I was scolded and advised that playing on unsafe ice displayed poor judgment.

*Dad's Houseboat on
Lake Cadillac (c. 1947)*

Brother Sigurd - 1953

Author - 1946

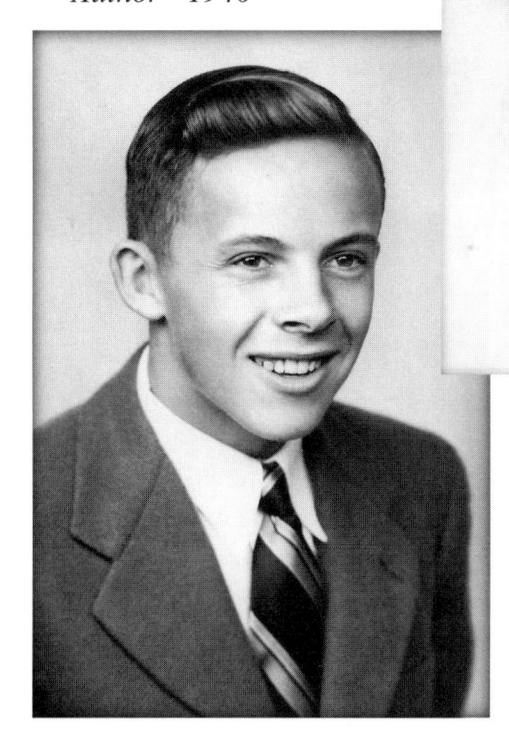

Pat - 1946

A SPECIAL AUNT AND UNCLE

When you look at your life, the greatest happiness's are family happiness's.
~ Joyce Brothers

Writing about sports and games provides me an opportunity to share some memories about my Mom's side of my family. Mom's older sister Pearl Hillard, and her husband, Will, lived on Carmel Street, near the eastern entrance to Cadillac. Uncle Will was a hard-working laborer while Aunt Pearl managed their childless home and maintained one of the most beautiful gardens in the community. She was an excellent cook and made cookies to die for. They would have been wonderful parents. They seemed to always be cheerful. I frequently stayed overnight at their home. With my new friends who resided in their neighborhood, I hiked and camped in nearby Bell's Woods.

I recall that Aunt Pearl did something with fried potatoes that even today makes me hungry for a serving. One of her favorite stories is the name I gave those mouth-watering treats. As a toddler, I once noticed that she put the left-over potatoes in Duke's dog dish. I labeled them "dog" potatoes. Forever after, Aunt Pearl with her high-pitched laugh would invite me for a plate of her "dog" potatoes. They always had a hound dog that was loved and treated very well and they were all named Duke.

Uncle Will was very good at baseball and played on some of Cadillac's best teams during the early 1900's. Our family and the Hillards spent many memorable days together in the woods picnicking and pursuing small game during those Great Depression years.

They enjoyed games of all kinds. They introduced me to caroms, a board game where one flips a small circular wooden disk with a finger to sink other same sized disks into side pockets on a 30" square board. That game has been handed down and is now played by my grandchildren.

Uncle Will made a beanbag board and Aunt Pearl made the bags, which provided many enjoyable hours casting the bags toward their target holes on the board. Aunt Pearl also taught me the games of Chinese checkers and cribbage, as well as several card games. Uncle Will tried to teach me how to box, but I failed to reach his expectations.

Aunt Pearl and Uncle Will were very important people in my life. They helped me learn the joy of competition, fair play, and how to win and lose with grace. Their significant contributions to my maturing process served me well.

COUSIN BOB AND THE EAGLE SCHOOL

The school is the last expenditure upon which America should be willing to economize.
~ Franklin D. Roosevelt

While on spring breaks during my early elementary school years my parents would take me to Ludington to stay with my favorite cousin, Bob Peterson, two years my senior. Bob, his parents Aunt Vivi and Uncle Bill, and his older siblings, Loraine and Bill, lived on a very nice farm about four miles east of Ludington near the one-room Eagle School.

Because it was an agricultural area, Eagle School students did not have a spring break, which enabled them to finish early and help plant the spring crops. During that week, I accompanied Bob across a small field to the one-room school where I thoroughly enjoyed attending classes. The teacher was very kind. She got me involved in class activities. One-room schools, while undoubtedly challenging for those creative and committed teachers, provided an unusually warm and nurturing learning environment for the students.

Eagle School had one teacher and about 25 students in grades one through eight. A wood-burning potbellied stove kept the building cozy warm. Students were seated in rows by grade level. The teacher shoveled the pathways near the school, cleaned the outdoor privy, started and maintained the heating stove, and cleaned the lunch debris so classes could commence. She made sure that everybody was properly clothed for the winter recess period, which was always held outside. The teacher was continually challenged to keep students with such varying age levels interested throughout the school day. Older students assisted younger students with their writing skills and numbers.

Ludington was a special place for me to be during my early years. Each summer, I would spend one or two weeks at the farm. Uncle Bill on his way to work at the Watch Case factory, would take Bob and me to the beautiful beach at the Ludington State Park where we would spend the entire day swimming, building sand castles, observing fishermen on the pier, and carefully spending our ten cents daily allotment on popcorn and a piece of candy.

The farm was a very interesting place for this city kid. It had a big barn, several smaller structures for stock and storage, an apple orchard, a well-maintained lawn surrounded by beautiful hardwoods and pines, and a pond in a small grove across a field where one could observe nature at work.

I enjoyed very much my Peterson relatives in Ludington. Loraine attended Michigan Normal College and was a teacher. Bill, after graduating from Michigan

State served as an officer in the US Navy as a Seabee during World War II. He owned a successful construction business in Ludington. Bill's construction crew built the Veteran's Memorial Stadium in Cadillac. Bob, a great high school athlete, remained in Ludington where he raised his son and two daughters.

My associations with the Petersons have enriched my life immeasurably.

CADILLAC HIGH SCHOOL AND THE "Y"

If you think education is expensive, try ignorance.
~ Attributed to both Andy McIntyre and Derek Bok

World War II began on December 7, 1941 when Japan launched an unprovoked attack on Pearl Harbor that was soon followed by a US declaration of war on Japan and Germany. At that time, I was an eighth grader at Cooley Grade School without any idea about the impact that terrible event would have on my life. I was more concerned about my future as a Cadillac High School freshman the following fall.

It was time to change my lifestyle. My neighborhood friends would need to find new playmates while my fellow eighth graders and I would face an uncertain future together. No more Kool-Aid stands and selling magazines, nor would I continue with my paper route.

My freshman year at CHS was a difficult year for me, probably the most wasted period in my life. With my pimpled face and skinny frame, I carried with me the notion that everybody was smarter than me. If only I could return to the friendly confines of Cooley where the teachers liked me and where I was always among friends.

I opted for easy courses and spent much of my classroom time watching the clock, hoping that I wouldn't be called upon to recite in class. My grades were average and I made few new friends. Adding to my angst was the considerable time spent in a dentist chair, where I experienced great fear and pain, the memories of which remain with me today. Nonetheless, I "survived" that year and, happily, found new life as a sophomore.

Much credit for my educational awakening goes to Mr. Sam Lee Nelson, my tenth grade World History teacher. It was the first high school class that I enjoyed. Mr. Nelson opened my eyes to the world beyond Cadillac and challenged me to think more in depth about other places and other peoples. It was also the class where I first saw a pretty girl who would later become my bride.

The walls of Mr. Nelson's first floor classroom were adorned with maps and posters depicting flags and other symbols of countries throughout the world. Each class would begin with a brief discussion on current events highlighting our country's progress on the battlefronts and sprinkled with comments on the plight of the common people in those war zones.

(Forgive me for employing that time-honored writer's privilege to boast a bit. The words that follow are offered to reveal how a teacher can have a profound influence on a student's future.)

Mr. Nelson instilled in me an enthusiasm for learning. I would daydream about exotic adventures in Cairo, Karachi, Katmandu, Caracas and other "faraway places with strange sounding names." After two years in college I joined the US Navy. My deployments included a few Caribbean countries followed by a six months' cruise in the Mediterranean Sea where my ship visited ports in Southern Europe, Turkey, and Algeria. Often, I would walk the streets of those port cities, usually alone, where I conversed with locals in shops, park benches, and at coffee counters. Europeans warmly received American service members during that post-World War II era. Mr. Nelson's words and classroom displays entered my thoughts frequently.

My first position after college was teaching history at Frankfort High School. Later as a college administrator I accepted many overseas consulting assignments that along with vacations with my wife brought me to more than 100 countries located throughout the earth's populated continents. Included among countless cities visited were Cairo, Karachi, Katmandu, and Caracas. My dream came true!

My doctorate at The University of Michigan centered on international education. I was either elected or appointed as a senior international education officer in three national professional organizations. I have written extensively on international education issues with some of my work translated into several languages.

Since 1993, after my second retirement, I continued to travel frequently as a volunteer for the International Baccalaureate Diploma Programme, a rigorous worldwide secondary school curriculum based in Geneva.

Finally, as a retiree in my hometown, I scanned, researched, and wrote descriptions for more than 1,500 early Wexford County photographs for the local historical society website. I narrated dozens of slide lectures on our area's colorful history throughout the community.

Can one teacher make a difference in the life of a student? Yes, he or she can! As a teacher, was I able to motivate my students to chase their dreams and achieve successes far beyond their expectations? I most certainly hope so!

Several years ago, I visited Mr. Nelson at his Suttons Bay lakeside home and thanked him for the positive impact that he had on my life. Although in his nineties, he still displayed that calm demeanor and the sparkling twinkle in his eyes that captivated his students.

I also enjoyed Mr. David Sjoberg's biology class that year, where I studied true science for the first time. He once complimented me in front of the class as one of the best dissectors of a frog. There I discovered that I could compete scholastically with college preparatory students and that I enjoyed their company.

I established friendships that would influence me to take the most difficult courses, particularly in mathematics and science, during my junior and senior years. Although I had to double up on those tough courses in my final two years, I still found time to participate in athletics, hold down a job, take part in several extra-curricular activities, and spend time with my friends virtually every night!

Another teacher who had a profound influence on my life was Mr. Edward Babcock, my chemistry and physics teacher. Mr. B was not only my teacher; he was my supervisor when I was a swimming instructor and lifeguard at Cadillac's Community Beach during my final two years of high school and my first two years at college. During those first two years, I also worked for him at the "Y." These were ideal jobs for me as I was surrounded by friends while learning life's lessons and earning money.

Most teachers at Cadillac High School during the war were women. They demanded good behavior in the classrooms and the hallways. When causing disruptions in class, the student was sent to the principal's office where penalties ranged from a mild reprimand and a return to the class, notes to parents, or detention after school.

A junior year teacher had her unique style of discipline. If a student was caught chewing gum in class, she made the offender place the gum on the end of his or her nose, there to rest for the remainder of the class period. Once when caught passing a note to a friend, I was instructed to draw a small circle on the blackboard and place my nose in the circle for a few minutes. One might think that she had some kind of a nose fetish.

My modest achievements in high school included one first place finish that never made it to my job-seeking resumes. I won a leg contest! During the fall tern of my senior year, about a dozen football players were gathered on the assembly hall stage with pant legs rolled up to mid-thigh and the stage curtain lowered to that same point. The entire student body voted with loud cheers for their favorites. Probably because I had been a swimming instructor during the summer, my well-tanned legs looked different. I retained the Cadillac Evening News item of the event.

Mr. Nelson, Mr. Sjoberg, Mr. Babcock and a host of other very good teachers by their patience and understanding, helped a shy young teenager overcome his anxieties and go on to achieve far beyond his expectations. It is no wonder that I chose education as my career. I had good role models.

Being relatively small and rather shy, I did not go out for sports at Cadillac High School until my junior year when my friend Jack Quinn convinced me to try out for the football team. I made the team (I think everybody did in those days) and enjoyed the experience, especially the camaraderie with the guys.

Alva Asbury was the new Viking head coach in fall 1945, my senior year. I started every game as quarterback. Coach Asbury introduced a new and complicated offense that I had to master quickly as the quarterback determined each play selection. I had to learn offense plays from several configurations that included the T-formation, split-T, single-wing, double wing, and Notre Dame box. I played linebacker and roving back on defense,

We had a winning, although not a great season. Because of wartime gas rationing, the four southern teams: Ludington, Manistee, Traverse City, and Cadillac, played each other twice and the winner played the northern team (Alpena, Cheboygan, Petoskey, or Rogers City) with the best record for the league championship.

The highlight of the year was our two games with archrival Traverse City Central. We defeated them six to zero in Cadillac and they won by the same score on their home field. The games were remarkably similar. In each game, the home team took the opening kick-off, moved the ball down the field for a touchdown, failed on the conversion attempt, and were outplayed the rest of the game. Those two games placed a special exclamation mark on arguably the fiercest and one of the longest sports rivalries in Northern Michigan that goes back to the late nineteenth century!

Facemasks came later!

The highlight of my varsity basketball experience was tying for high point honors in our game with Traverse City. The Trojans beat us 52 to 14. A teammate and I both scored three points which, if such records are kept, we may have set a standard in futility for the fewest points scored by the leading scorers. Our basketball team won only two games that year. Winter was for skiing and hockey. We had the wrong mind-set for the hoops.

Coach Asbury convinced me to go out for track my senior year. The sport was of little interest to me, but it was another opportunity to be with my friends. I was somewhat successful having never lost a race in the conference and winning the regional competition.

Although I qualified for the state meet in East Lansing, I barely met the academic standard of CHS. A senior year physics project was to construct a motor, literally from the "ground up." I was among a few students who were unable to complete the assignment on time.

It was late Friday afternoon, the day before the "states". Mr. B remained after school with me for a final attempt. Surrounded by some of my teammates, I assembled and re-assembled my crude machine three or four times before it began its very slow movement. To the applause of my friends, its rotation speed slowly increased and finally settled into a heartwarming purr. I could pack for the states where I placed either third or fourth in the 880- yard run.

Obviously, Dad did not share with me his good mechanical genes! Engineering was quickly removed as a college option.

After turning down an invitation by the track coach to attend Michigan State College (MSU) I enrolled at Central Michigan College (later CMU.) Once again, to be with my friends was a priority. I lettered in track at Central running both the half-mile and the mile runs, as well as the relays.

I still have my yellow and blue T-shirt with the classical Viking warrior head and the words, "Take a Liking to a Viking."

The Cadillac Youth Recreation Association (The "Y")

"See ya at the `Y` tonight!" was a phrase heard frequently throughout the halls of the old Cadillac High School during the mid- 1940's.

The former Young Men's Christian Association (YMCA) four-story structure built in 1908 was located on the southwest corner of Mitchell and Chapin streets. It closed during the 1930's and re-opened during World War II as the Cadillac Youth Recreation Association (CYRA.) The huge building was razed around 1990.

In late 1943 a group of citizens assembled to plan a recreational program for the young people of Cadillac. Mr. Babcock, my CHS science teacher, was appointed manager. I was one of the first student staff members at the 'Y." I deeply regret that a similar venue does not exist for today's youth.

The building included a gymnasium for volleyball and basketball, bowling alleys, and a swimming pool. The pool was not operational. Popular activities included ping-pong and pool tables, board games, intramural basketball games, and Friday night dances after the CHS varsity games. The wartime recreational program also included management of ice-skating at Diggins Park and a varied program of supervised swimming and lifesaving instruction at Community Beach. Students from throughout the city were transported to the beach.

Some evenings would see hundreds of students participating in the various activities at the "Y."

Mr. B depended on the student staff to plan and lead nearly all activities. That level of responsibility was a great leadership experience for us. We managed the basketball schedules, recruited the officials and score keepers, and kept track of the equipment. We made sure that there was a proper rotation of players at the very popular ping-pong and pool tables.

Cadillac High School did not have a girls varsity basketball program during those days, but there were many very good girl athletes. One day we challenged the best girl athletes to a game played under their rules. In their game, a team consisted of six players, three in the frontcourt (offensive) and three in the backcourt (defensive.) Players had to remain in the assigned courts. A dribble could not exceed two bounces. In place of jump balls, the teams would alternate throw-ins from the sidelines. As I recall we lost. They probably beat us by free throws. We kept running over the centerline!

During my experiences at the "Y," I got to know well many fellow students who I passed daily in the school's halls without notice. The 'Y' had many varied activities that gave participants an opportunity to find one or more in which they excelled. While I didn't realize it at the time, the place was a confidence builder. Whether it's ping pong, pool, dancing, volleyball or any one of several activities, most students probably left the building with a smile on their face knowing that they competed successfully.

The success of the "Y" can be attributed to the fact that the program was based on democratic principles and that students had a major role in the decision-making.

Best Friend: Jack Quinn

*Favorite Teacher:
Sam Lee Nelson*

My Three
Athletic C's

*Cooley Grade School
(red & white)
Cadillac High School
(blue & gold)*

*Central Michigan College
(maroon & gold)*

Cadillac High School Vikings varsity (1945)
Author No. 40 (Quarterback)

Central Michigan College
Track Team Members
Author – first row, left. c.1947

Author-U.S. Navy
c. 1952

CADILLAC DURING THE WAR YEARS

In war, there are no unwounded soldiers.
~ José Narosky

Most of my high school years came during World War II. It was a difficult time for America as our country was engaged in major armed conflicts on two fronts, Europe and East Asia.

Patriotism was rampant. Nobody questioned our national commitment to defeat the aggressor nations of Japan and Germany. Some of us were mildly disappointed when the war ended before we had the opportunity to serve.

People did not complain about food and gasoline rationing, air raid drills, and other inconveniences as we realized that the fighting men and women of the military forces were the ones who made the true sacrifices. The international situation of the times brought us all together and community-wide thoughtfulness and understanding had a substantial influence on our behaviors. Many suffered the loss of a family member, friend, or neighbor in the war. More than 1,800 Wexford County servicemen and women served in World War II. According to the local American Legion Post 94, more than 90 warriors made the supreme sacrifice.

Crime and neighbor squabbles were rare. Because of the lack of manpower in the community everybody was busy. Many teenagers assumed adult roles and responsibilities, giving our generation a head start on the maturation process. It was reported that the number of women occupying traditional male positions in Cadillac's factories went from near zero to about 800 during the war years.

In many ways, it was a good time to grow up and prepare for life's next challenges. Unfortunately, all too many brave Americans died so that the rest of us could pursue our dreams. To those warriors, I owe my most sincere appreciation.

LCVP (Landing Craft Vehicle Personnel.) During World War II, over 2,000 were made by the Chris-Craft Boat Co. in Cadillac, Michigan.

Center Theatre, North Mitchell St

*Cooley Grade School
Built in the 1920's
(Photo taken Jan. 2016)*

*Cadillac High School
(Constructed in 1889. Wings added in 1912)*

EMPLOYMENT DURING MY HIGH SCHOOL YEARS

While earning your daily bread be sure you share a slice with those less fortunate.
~ H. Jackson Brown, Jr.

The summer following my eighth grade (1942,) I secured a job at Louis Present's Style Shop on South Mitchell Street, where I swept floors, prepared stock, and washed display windows. My friends always seemed to be passing by when I was in the store display window assisting one of the clerks while she installed a garment on a mannequin! It was my first job working under direct supervision and I got along just fine.

As a tenth grader, I worked at Woolley's Drug Store doing many odd jobs including general maintenance, clerking, and serving customers at the soft drink bar.

Those work experiences were very important in my early development. Both managers were demanding albeit caring individuals. With a pleasant home life and a rather comfortable grade school experience, I was now facing the real world where I became a participant in a local business' drive for financial gain and providing services to customers.

My eleventh grade was the year that I landed an ideal job. The city arranged for the vacated YMCA ("Y") building on South Mitchell Street to become the Cadillac Youth Recreation Association (CYRA).

Several teenagers were recruited to work the concession counter, organize activities, officiate basketball games, teach pool and ping-pong, and perform routine maintenance tasks, such as cleaning and painting. I once stood precariously on the second story window ledge to wash the upper outside pane. I still shudder a bit as I write this today,

At the "Y" we could have fun, unleash our creative juices, and get paid. Edward Babcock, a teacher, was the supervisor. He depended on student help to select and plan the activities that would be most appropriate for our age group. We even provided vocal entertainment, Karaoke style, as we spun records and sang along with the recording artist for the Friday and Saturday night dances in the gym. I worked at the CYRA for two years.

My junior year also launched me into a four-year summer job as a Water Safety Instructor (WSI) and lifeguard at the Community Beach on Lake Cadillac. To be certified to teach swimming and lifesaving, I was sent to the WSI Aquatic School at Lake Minnetonka, Excelsior, Minnesota, as no spots were available in Michigan.

My parents drove me to the Grand Rapids airport where I embarked on my first commercial airplane trip. I managed Midway Airport in Chicago without a mishap. At the next stop, thinking that I was in Minnesota, I left the plane to get the bus to the swim camp. When told that I was in Madison, Wisconsin, a red cap ushered me quickly back to my plane just in time to make the continuing flight to my destination. In the estimated two to three million miles I've flown since that fateful day, I never again made that mistake.

As one of the youngest trainees and one of only a few boys at the camp, I prepared myself to teach swimming in Lake Cadillac.

That summer, buses would bring hundreds of children to Community Beach each day. Our staff of 8 to 10 teenagers taught swimming and lifesaving at all levels. We organized beach games for the children. We also borrowed city trucks and hauled many yards of sand from a nearby wooded area to expand the beach size. Many vacationers from cottages, as well as adults from the area, gave us a diverse and interesting population to watch over and occasionally date during the summer months.

At the beach, Jack Quinn and I chose to launch a "tradition." We swam from the beach to the city dock. As far as I know, that "tradition" lasted one year.

My major winter "work" during my final two years in high school and my first two years in college had me as a member of Caberfae's ski patrol. We were paid $10 a day and I received an extra $2.50 to retrieve splints and other first aid devices from Mercy Hospital on Saturday nights.

With my athletics, work, and a rather active social life, my schoolwork suffered, although I did manage to do C+ to B- work. Cadillac had very good teachers and the academic and social skills I learned at CHS served me well in my future endeavors.

CENTRAL MICHIGAN COLLEGE OF EDUCATION

If you have a college degree you can be absolutely sure of one thing... you have a college degree.
~ Author Unknown

I graduated from Cadillac High School in 1946 with average grades thereby limiting my college choices. Because I successfully completed all of the school's college preparatory math and science courses, I was convinced that I could handle college level work.

The fall following my graduation from Cadillac High School in 1946, I entered Central Michigan College of Education (now Central Michigan University) where I opted for secondary education concentrations in physical education and history. My good friends, Jack Quinn and Jim Kearney, along with Wendell, a very nice farm boy from Perrinton, Michigan, and I shared an estimated 350 square foot room, number 106, in the Keeler Union men's dormitory.

I enjoyed college although nearly every weekend during our first two years, Jack and I would hitchhike home to serve on the Caberfae ski patrol, play softball on the Cap's Paint Store team, hunt deer or small game, take in the many activities at the Cadillac Youth Center, and hang out with friends.

I competed as an 880-yard middle distance runner on the track team. In dual meets, I almost always placed second in the 880, never able to beat teammate Jim Little. I also ran a mile leg on the four-mile relay team and a 440-yard leg on the mile relay squad. Our relay teams captured first place in several meets.

I failed in my attempt to make the CMCE football team. It was 1946 and the campus had a huge enrollment of returned World War II veterans that included some very good athletes and well-conditioned football players. I weighed 160 pounds at the time! I lasted about two weeks.

During my sophomore year I was selected for charter membership in the Delta Sigma Phi fraternity where many of those veterans became my good friends.

In September 1948 after two years of average grades at CMCE, I entered the US Navy. I needed a break from studies and time to think more seriously about my future.

I re-enrolled at Central two weeks after my 1952 USN Honorable Discharge. The first term I shared an apartment near campus with two Cadillac friends, Gus Thompson and Bud Oliver. After the first semester, I moved to the Delta Sigma Phi fraternity house. As before, most weekends were spent in Cadillac. I continued service on the Caberfae ski patrol. After my junior year, Pat and I were married and lived in a 28-foot house trailer, first in Midland where Pat taught at Carpenter School, and later in Mt. Pleasant while I completed by undergraduate degree in secondary education in June 1954.

The first two years of my undergraduate performance were satisfactory. After four years of military service, my final two years were much better. My MA and PhD record was markedly better, but grade inflation is traditionally applied at the graduate level.

ALPINE SKIING

*There is no cure for birth and
death save to enjoy the interval.*
~ George Santayana

My favorite sport has always been and remains to this day downhill skiing. I cannot recall my first experience on skis, although I have seen a photograph taken when I was three or four years of age sliding down our very short front yard terrace on two-foot skis.

My skiing interest was greatly enhanced during my junior year at Cadillac High School when I was invited to join the National Ski Patrol at the Caberfae Ski Area. I served on the patrol for ten years between 1944 and 1958, which were interrupted by US Navy service from 1948 to 1952. During the 1940's, the era of un-groomed slopes, un-releasable bindings, and little emphasis on safety instruction, patrol personnel were kept very busy on the hills. We retrieved injured skiers by toboggan, as snowmobiles would come much later.

Among my duties were Saturday and Sunday evening visits to Cadillac's Mercy Hospital to gather up and return to Caberfae the numerous splints and other medical supplies used to protect injured skiers on their trip to the hospital from Caberfae. On a Saturday of terrible snow conditions, nurses reported to me that 18 skiers with bone fractures had been treated!

My competitive skiing activities yielded but two recognitions. Skiing for Central Michigan, I won the intercollegiate downhill race at Caberfae in 1947. Today, however, they would most likely place an asterisk after my name. The Clare Manufacturing Company, together with Dow Chemical of Midland, designed and produced skis made entirely of aluminum with small toe-mounted prongs that anchored the ski to the boot. To test the skis for the

Clare manufacturer, ski patrol members were able to purchase a pair for six dollars, including bindings.

It was a cold, blustery day and Michigan State had a hotshot racer who was seldom beaten in downhill competition. Racing down Caberfae's Number One slope, I felt confident that I had a chance at coming in second. As I faced the timers at the completion of my run, I noted that they were comparing their stopwatch readings with wonderment. They checked with the folks at the starting gate and all seemed proper. After my equally successful second run the race officials discovered the reason: My new aluminum skis! On the unusually cold snow, the aluminum skis offered virtually no resistance while even well waxed wood skis were slower. On warm days, my aluminum skis would sometimes stop in the middle of the slope, as the aluminum is a great heat conductor.

The following year while I was away in the Navy, I suspect aluminums were banned from competition. I gave them to my Dad who used them to pull his fish shanty to his favorite holes on Lake Cadillac.

My other recognition was also achieved at Caberfae. The Bonne Bell Women's Cosmetic Company sponsored giant slalom races and I placed second in my age group. There I stood at the awards table, a single guy receiving a headscarf filled with all kinds of lotions, creams, and powders created to make a woman beautiful. Of course that prize never made it to the trophy case.

While living in Harbor Springs (1958 – 1960) as a high school teacher, I was hired as the first ski instructor at Nub's Nob, a very good northern Michigan slope. During my two years there I helped Norman

("Nub") and Doris Sarns lay out some of the initial runs. I also taught skiing to a large number of their Great Lakes sailing friends from the Detroit area and other slope skiers. Weekday nights I was sponsored by the Petoskey News to teach skiing across the valley from Nub's Nob at Boyne Highlands,

My skiing interests have taken me to resorts in the mountains of Colorado (Aspen, Breckenridge, Steamboat, Vail, Aspen Highlands, Snowmass, Keystone, Copper, A Basin, Winter Park), Utah (Alta, Park City, Snowbird), California (Mammoth, Squaw Valley, Sugar Loaf, Heavenly, Bear Mountain), and New Mexico (Taos and Santa Fe).

International slopes conquered included those in Chile (La Parva), Iran (Dizin), Norway (Geilo), Switzerland (St. Moritz and Montreaux), and France (Auron). My Switzerland and France adventures occurred in 1951-52 while serving on the USS Tarawa, an aircraft carrier cruising the Mediterranean Sea.

In Michigan, I have skied at Caberfae, Nub's Nob, Hickory Hills, Holiday Hills, Boyne Mt., Boyne Highlands, Snow Snake, Crystal Mountain, Mount Brighton, and a small "bump" on the landscape near Kalamazoo.

JACK, MY BEST FRIEND

> *A friend is one of the nicest things you can have, and one of the best things you can be.*
> ~ Douglas Pagels

As I look back over a rather happy and successful life, I have attempted to identify those individuals along the way who have had the greatest influence on me. Of course, Mom and Dad, my spouse, brother, and our four children, were all central figures in my 88-year march to and through adulthood. A grandmother, three aunts and two uncles impacted my personality in countless good ways. I can name five or six educators from the elementary through graduate levels that motivated me and supplied me with the confidence and the means to stretch myself intellectually and socially.

Along the way, a few other individuals stand out as having a significant impact on my life. Jack Quinn was one who captured my admiration early. I often wonder what kind of a person I would have become had Jack not entered my life during my freshman year in high school.

As a shy ninth grade student at Cadillac High School, I was a clock-watcher on a general course of studies, envious of my classmates who seemed always to be having fun. I can't recall exactly how Jack, a popular, confident, active guy, came into my life, but I think that one afternoon I timed my departure from school with Jack's. We both followed the same route home, although my trek was about twice as long. A pattern developed that led to a profound personal chemistry between us. As I wheeled my bike along the sidewalk while talking with Jack, I began to feel that maybe life wasn't so bad after all.

Early on, Jack talked me into taking more challenging courses, mostly in math and science. Chemistry, physics, trig, solid geometry? Ugh! I admired Jack, so I would do it! That meant that I would be in some classes with students a year younger than me, which probably contributed to an increased self-confidence. He convinced me to go out for sports. I lettered in football, basketball, and track. I was the quarterback and Jack was a receiver on the CHS football team. Jack and I both placed third in the state track finals in East Lansing, Jack in the 440-yard dash and I in the half-mile. Coincidence?

Jack and I lived in the south side of town. Both of us had really nice girlfriends who were north siders (both lived on Farrar Street.) We walked together to

Farrar Street to greet them, walk them back to the south side to the Youth Center or Lyric theatre, then back to their place and back home. The evening concluded with an hour, or so, conversation on the grassy northeast corner of Howard and South Mitchell streets.

It was during World War II and we talked about joining the US Navy Air Corps and maybe shoot down a few enemy aircraft. The conversations rambled on sometimes to early mornings.

Those long and pleasantly memorable walks not only proved to be great conditioning activities to prepare us for our athletic participation, but we learned how to adjust to the cold and snowy weather of Cadillac winters.

We worked together in the newly opened Youth Center and taught swimming and lifesaving at Community Beach. We served on the Caberfae Ski Patrol together. Jack and I were team members of the first nationally recognized Au Sable Canoe Marathon in 1947.

We attended college and roomed together for two years, after which both of us left for the US Navy, Jack to Officers Training School and I to the Great Lakes Navy Training Center as an enlistee.

End of story? Not yet! I was assigned to the US Naval Air Station, Boca Chica, Florida (near Key West) as an aerial photographer. One day, there was an unexpected visitor to the photo lab. It was Jack! He had been assigned as a pilot with FAWTU (Fleet All Weather Training Unit) and would be at Boca Chica for several months. (Coincidently, as an aerial photographer I was trained as a tail gunner in case our TBM Avenger was attacked.) We enjoyed each other's company and he continued to help me make the right decisions.

After two years at Boca Chica, I was assigned to the USS Tarawa, CV-40, an Essex-class aircraft carrier that operated out of Boston. During the fall of 1951, soon after we departed the US for a Mediterranean Sea cruise, I was assigned flight deck duty to photograph aircraft as they practiced "touch-downs" in the mid-Atlantic. Hundreds of planes arrived and launched, but one caught my eye. Jack, with his name emblazoned at the entry to his F-4U Corsair, had landed on the USS Tarawa. We enjoyed many "liberties" together in Istanbul, Athens, Barcelona, the beaches of France, and elsewhere during our seven-month Mediterranean deployment.

The story continues. While I was admissions director at the UM in the 1970's, I was invited to Princeton, New Jersey, to help select outstanding high school students for US Navy-sponsored NROTC scholarships. It was a rigorous process. Among the applications I reviewed was Jack's son, who was attending high school in North Carolina. I convinced my committee colleagues that this young man was from very good stock. He was awarded a scholarship.

After a highly successful navy career, Jack entered the sales force of a major international corporation. I knew that he would be successful. He sold me on the many ways to enjoy a productive life.

By the way, we married Betty and Pat, those "really nice girlfriends." And one more coincidence; we were both born in the Highland Park Hospital near Detroit!

JAIL TIME

It's nice to be important, but it's more important to be nice.
~ Author Unknown

I have experienced more than 32,000 nights of sleep in my life, but only one has been in a jail.

Best friend Jack Quinn and I, then sophomores at Central Michigan College, spent a Friday evening in our dorm listening to a Joe Louis fight. The "Brown Bomber," a Michigander, was the world heavyweight champion and his fights seldom lasted more than a few rounds.

Most weekends we hitchhiked to Cadillac to be with friends, although most departures were at an earlier time. With our dirty clothes for our moms to wash, we stepped out on Mission Street in Mt. Pleasant to hitch a ride to Cadillac. By 10:00 PM we were on our familiar corner in downtown Clare. An hour later, we were still at that corner. There were few cars on the road at that hour.

About a block up US-10 towards our destination we noticed bright lights. We entered the County Sheriff's office and jail and found no one on duty. After waiting about 30 minutes we noticed that the door to the jail cells was ajar. We peeked in the cell area and found it unpopulated. Assuming the on-duty police officer was on patrol, we each picked out a cell and promptly fell asleep.

Early the following morning a smiling sheriff with eggs, bacon, and a glass of milk awakened us. After we complimented him on the cleanliness of his jail, the quality of our breakfast, followed by many "thanks'" for his kindness, we continued our way north,

If by chance I ever spend another night in jail, I hope that it's in Clare, Michigan! It was a "five-star facility!"

"JACK, WHY...?"

Optimism is the foundation of courage.
                    ~ Nicholas Murray Butler

The first Au Sable River Canoe Marathon departed from Grayling in September 1947. My friend Jack Quinn and I entered that competition. My essay that follows was later edited by a friend, a Detroit Free Press retiree in Traverse City, and published as a Feature in the Traverse City regional monthly newspaper, "Prime Time: News & Observer," July 1997. I was also invited that year to discuss my experience in Grayling at the 50th anniversary of that popular event.

Jack Quinn was my best friend. We participated in high school and college sports together, worked at the same beach as swimming instructors, and even dated girls from the same part of town. Later, we were assigned to the same US Navy base and aircraft carrier.

Jack had many highly desirable characteristics, but the two that nearly drove me mad was his unbridled optimism and his determination to take on what I considered to be unreasonable challenges. I wasn't quite sure just how far Jack would go with his adventurous spirit until an event scheduled for a Northern Michigan river invaded his thoughts.

It was late summer, 1947. We had completed our freshman year at Central Michigan College and were working at the Community Beach in our hometown of Cadillac. One evening, Jack showed me a brochure that described what was to be the first Au Sable River Canoe Marathon. We read that the course consisted of about 240 miles of paddling (if you took the most efficient route), portages around six dams, and a number of backwaters characterized by slow water and dead-end coves. (Later the length of the course was adjusted to a more accurate reading of 120 miles.) It was to begin in Grayling during an afternoon and finish in Oscoda at Lake Huron sometime the next afternoon. It was a race that would require endurance, skills, strength, and, yes, Jack's optimism and determination.

Jack said, "Let's do it."

I replied, "Jack, why?"

"Because I know that we can win it."

I had always admired Jack's can-do attitude and found it to be somewhat contagious. I said yes. During the following few weeks, while we continued to teach children how to swim in Lake Cadillac, we attempted to prepare ourselves mentally for a competition about which we knew little.

Most of our canoe activity had been on the Manistee and Pine rivers, the latter of which had provided us with many exhilarating "white water" experiences. College track competition and swimming had kept us in reasonably good physical shape and we were loaded with confidence! Although we had never dipped a paddle in the Au Sable, we had mastered the Pine, which was widely acknowledged among canoeists as one of Michigan's more perilous rivers. How could the Au Sable be tougher? We would find out. Today, one might call those who would undertake such an activity without being properly prepared as "common sense challenged!" Our friends simply said that we were "nuts."

Our registration and five dollar entry fee had been sent and we began the search for a canoe. We talked to Gus Holman, the canoe liveryman at the Canal between lakes Cadillac and Mitchell. We were advised that all of his canoes were committed for the Labor Day weekend. Oh, my! Was our entry fee wasted? Never fear! Jack is here!

"We will find a canoe on our way to Grayling," he stated with his typical air of confidence that clearly lacked caution.

My Dad loaned us his pick-up truck and we headed for Grayling. As Jack had predicted, we found a canoe in back of a small sports shop in Kalkaska. It was an aged wood and canvas craft, about 18 feet long that revealed its many years of use and abuse by its weight. We immediately named it "Old War Horse." We had our canoe and we headed east to Grayling where we would show others how Pine River paddlers navigate treacherous waters.

We arrived at the race area parking lot and, with hundreds of race spectators curiously watching, dragged Old War Horse to the river's edge. Other entrants carried their canoes. Were they stronger than we were? We checked in and waited our turn for the staggered start. We learned that there were 48 entrants, which included many experienced racers. It will be fun to compete with these guys, we thought.

Minutes after we splashed down in the river, we knew we were in a bit of trouble. Dampness appeared inside the canoe. Then water. After an hour of paddling, the candy bars I brought for energy begin to float in the bottom of our craft.

"No problem," said Jack. "Remember, we've handled the Pine and we can certainly handle this softy." I emptied my bottle of fresh water from home so I could use it to bale Au Sable water out of our canoe.

A most enduring memory of the race was the spectators who lined the banks along the way. Many thoughtful folks stood on the low bridges and cheered us on as they dropped sandwiches in passing canoes. They were rather good "bombardiers." We heard the "plops" as the sandwiches hit the canoe decks of other race entrants near us. Unfortunately, their good aim resulted in a "splash" in our canoe and I was forced to watch my Baby Ruth's float with peanut butter and jelly sandwiches, at least until we got around the next bend. Nuts! Why didn't "optimistic and determined" Jack take the stern, so he could carry lifetime guilt feelings about littering one of America's most beautiful rivers with wax paper wrapped sandwiches?

It was a long day and a longer night. We soon found that our white water canoeing experience was of little help. What we needed were skills on how to avoid slightly submerged logs, overhanging branches, and rocky sandbars while paddling in unfamiliar waters in darkness! Approaching a dam, the Mio Dam, I believe, we followed the lights instead of the natural river current and got lost in some lengthy coves. That's when I first suggested to Jack that maybe we should pull out. Fat chance. "Remember the Pine!"

We had been counting canoes that passed us and figured that there were at least 20 behind us. What we didn't know was that most of those had already given up and were probably sleeping or eating, either of which I would have gladly accepted at the time. We backtracked and found our way to the next portage, disembarked, emptied the water out of our canoe, and dragged it on to the river below the dam.

After about 25 hours on the river, numbness was setting in. I became angry with Jack, calling him stubborn and insensitive to my sleep and nourishment needs. And he was angry with me. He accused me of not paddling as hard as he was. Ah, ha! There was an advantage to paddling stern. Then we gave each other the "silent" treatment and all went well while we eagerly anticipated Oscoda.

As we paddled the slow waters of the Foote Dam Pond not far from the finish line, we became energized and experienced a surge of excitement. We had done it! Those 20 guys were still behind us. Old War Horse" had brought us through after all and we would finish no worse than 28th!

The 120-mile river (probably 150 miles for us!) was indeed a challenge, and while the experience was nothing like the sprints down the Pine, the Au Sable marathon most certainly proved to be a formidable task.

We felt emotionally charged as we prepared ourselves to acknowledge the adulations of the throngs who would be at the river's edge and cheer us on to the finish line.

But, alas! No one was there. After dragging our water soaked canoe to the shore in Oscoda, we walked to the race desk where the event officials were folding their tables and packing away their papers. They were quite surprised to see us, to say the least. We had been on the river for over 30 hours in a race that was won in a time of about 24 hours. Only 12 of the 48 entrants completed the race and our last place finish was about three hours behind the 11th place canoe! Nonetheless, we were rewarded with the complimentary chicken dinner for race finishers. With our blistered hands wrapped in gauze, we dined alone.

We left Old War Horse on the river's bank, fully confident that it would not be stolen. We hitchhiked to Grayling to get Dad's pick-up and deliver that leaky, water-soaked mass of canvas and wood back to its owner.

Was the grueling paddle down the Au Sable River a valuable experience? I think it was. A finish among the top quarter of all entrants was a highly satisfying achievement for us. (Must we qualify that by saying that we were the last finishers?) And might we assume that no one since has completed the Au Sable race with a heavier canoe? Probably. Many of today's sleek racing canoes are closer to the weight of my 1947 stern paddle than to the weight of Old War Horse. Obviously, this essay suggests that, if not valuable, it was at least an unforgettable experience.

As I reflect back on the 1947 experience, many emotions come into play. I'm not sure if or how our participation in that historic event had made any differences in our lives. Jack, who died at an all-too-early age, had all the personal qualities to be a leader and a model in just about any field of endeavor. He chose the military and completed a highly successful career as a U S Navy pilot, while raising a family of unusual abilities and good character. And I know that my time with Jack Quinn, both on and off the Au Sable River, has positively influenced my life.

    My wish is that I could again pose the oft-asked question to my good friend. "Jack, why?"

PART TWO: MOVING ON

My life changed abruptly at age 21. On September 1, 1948, it was "good-bye" carefree life and "hello" adulthood! I had joined the Navy. Actually, one might say it was a dichotomy. I left an environment of fun and freedom and responsibility for my actions to a highly restricted one where it seemed that my every move was ordered or expected by other people. My thinking process was replaced by obeying the orders. Standards of behavior that made no sense to me were applied. Welcome to the US Navy "boot camp."

US NAVY SERVICE

Though we travel the world over to find the beautiful, we must carry it with us or we find it not.
~ Ralph Waldo Emerson

My four years in the US Navy (September 1, 1948 to September 3, 1952) proved to be a positive experience for me (except "boot camp.") After two years in college, I remained undecided about a life career. With two Cadillac friends, Jim Kearney and Gus Thompson, I enlisted and was assigned to the Great Lakes Naval Training Center in Illinois. Because of satisfactory test scores and college attendance, I was invited to apply for USN Officers' Training School. However, those first few weeks of "boot camp" were unpleasantly restrictive and left me less than pleased with the USN so I declined.

KEY WEST AND PENSACOLA

The love of one's country is a splendid thing. But why should love stop at the border?
~ Pablo Casals

Following "boot camp," I was asked where I would like to serve. I thought what a nice thing to do and listed, "overseas in a northern country." "Ha!" I was billeted to the Boca Chica Naval Air base located about seven miles from Key West, Florida!

There I became an aerial photographer for VX-1, one of the Navy's premier experimental flight centers. Happily, the photo lab was one of only a few air-conditioned workstations at Boca Chica.

My flight time at Boca Chica was in many types of aircraft, including two-man torpedo bombers, high altitude attack bombers, reconnaissance planes, helicopters, and dirigibles (blimps). Most of my time was spent in the base photo lab learning photography, processing film, and printing photos.

I played a lot of tennis and represented VX-1 in the Atlantic Fleet finals in Jacksonville where I was eliminated in the first round. I made many good friends at the base, especially Terry of Beloit, Wisconsin, Joe of East Boston, and Steve, of West Palm Beach, Florida. I was best man at Kenny's wedding (Missouri.)

A highlight of my Key West deployment was a salute from a US President. I was assigned security at a rural road between the base and Key West. When President Harry Truman rode by my post in his convertible heading for his winter retreat in Key West, he returned my snappy salute with a wave of his hand and a very warm smile.

Liberty (time off base) was spent in Key West, Miami, and occasional flights to Havana and Guantanamo Bay in Cuba. Key West, at that time, was a wide-open frontier-type town of several dozen bars, nightclubs, tattoo parlors, and illegal gambling joints.

Weekends during the summer in Miami Beach, Fort Lauderdale, and Palm Beach allowed us to enjoy life as tourists. During the off-season, ocean side hoteliers would rent us rooms for two dollars a night. The base supplied buses to transport us the 140 miles to Miami. Civilians treated sailors with much respect in those post-World War II days.

In July 1949, I was deployed to the aerial photography school in Pensacola, Florida for six months of training. I passed with flying colors and even won a ping-pong match while in the base hospital with my leg in a cast. (I beat a guy in a wheel chair with short drop shots just over the net!)

I returned to Key West in January 1950 and resumed my duties with my squadron. Upon my return, memorable experiences included flying above and photographing into the eye of a hurricane (the photos appeared in Life Magazine.)

THE USS TARAWA, CV-40

If you are ashamed to stand by your colors, you had better seek another flag.
~ Author Unknown

After two years in Florida, I was assigned to the re-commissioned USS Tarawa, CV-40, an Essex-class aircraft carrier afloat in the South Boston Navy Yard. Our ship was "adopted" by the State of Connecticut and I was one of the ship's photographers assigned to record the ceremonies on film.

Our shakedown cruise was in the Caribbean Sea with port visits in Haiti and Cuba. That was followed by a seven-month cruise to several ports in the Mediterranean Sea.

One of my primary responsibilities was to stand on the flight deck and photograph with a 16mm movie camera any difficulties encountered by departing or returning aircraft. Occasionally I would be assigned a helicopter duty and record flight deck actions from above. I witnessed and recorded a number of accidents, some of which were quite serious.

A secondary assignment, which was to add immeasurably to my bank of Navy experiences, was the responsibility for the control and distribution of permanent and expendable materials in the ship's photo laboratory storeroom.

Clearly, a highlight of my life was that experience aboard the USS Tarawa, fondly labeled the "Terrible T." Because of my highly classified work, I was cleared for "Top Secret" assignments. During this period I was an Aerial Photographer Petty Officer Third Class. Just prior to my Honorable discharge I was promised promotion to P. O. Second Class if I re-enlisted.

The ship, with its crew of 2,800 men and about 100 aircraft, including a few jets, departed Rhode Island in early December 1951 for the Mediterranean Sea deployment. A severe Atlantic storm delayed the Gibraltar arrival date by two days.

It was during the Korean War. The USS Tarawa was responsible for patrolling the area with an eye on our cold war rival, the Union Soviet Socialist Republic (Russia) as well as carry out intelligence and aerial photographic operations of landmasses and ports around the eastern Mediterranean Sea areas.

We visited twenty ports during the assignment that included the following countries: France, Algeria, Spain, Greece, Italy (and Sicily,) Turkey, Crete, Sardinia, Mallorca (Spain,) and Gibraltar. The Navy employed what was termed "three section liberty," one-day liberty, one-day duty, and one-day standby. I was fortunate: I went ashore for fun on liberty, as duty photographer on standby, and as shore patrol on duty! We were in port about a third of the time. My experiences included: Skiing at Auron, France and St. Moritz and Montreux, Switzerland; four days in Venice; a trip to an oasis village in the Algerian desert; and a tour of Pompeii. Because it was so soon after World War II, the various populations treated us very well.

The St. Moritz ski experience was indeed memorable. Four officers accompanied me on the tour from the USS Tarawa. From the highest point on the ski slope, we could see the village of St. Moritz far below. A silly thought entered my mind. Before sanity returned, I pointed my seven-foot skis toward the village with a plan to ski to the hotel. That plan was shattered about one-half of the way toward my destination as I found myself in a snowless farmer's pasture. With ski boots on my feet and the seven-foot skis thrust over my shoulder, I scaled a few fences where I was observed by some curious cows and a few friendly bulls. After an hour of walking on grass, my somewhat worried shipmates greeted me in darkness with wide smiles.

The USS Wasp, our intended relief, collided with the destroyer escort, the USS Hobson, during their

Atlantic Ocean crossing to the Mediterranean Sea. One hundred and seventy-six Hobson sailors perished in the accident. The Wasp was forced to return to its US port and our cruise was extended six additional weeks to mid-June 1952.

  My parents, brother Sig and his friend, Lynn Johnson, traveled to Quonset Point, Rhode Island, to greet me soon after I returned to the US. Because I was to be discharged soon, Dad loaded much of my gear, including my two pairs of Attenhofer skis purchased in Switzerland for my brother, Sig, and me, onto and on top of the car for their long trip home. Very few people skied in those days and Sig noted the many curious stares along the way. I also purchased two Italian Beretta pistols, a 22 and a 32 caliber and a number of souvenirs. I was discharged September 3, 1952 and immediately re-enrolled as a junior at Central Michigan College to complete my undergraduate studies.

Photo # NH 97596   USS Tarawa underway north of the Straits of Messina, Sicily, December 1952

Author skiing at St. Moritz, Switzerland while serving on the USS Tarawa (CV- 40) 1952

Author. Aerial Photographer USN

COURTSHIP AND MARRIAGE

*A friend is one who knows you
and loves you just the same*
~ Elbert Hubbard

The country was deeply involved in World War II during that fall in 1943 when, in Mr. Nelson's tenth grade World History class, I first noticed Pat Chick. Too shy to approach her (or any girl!) I was nonetheless taken in by her pleasant demeanor and engaging smile. It would be the following school year that a relationship began, albeit off and on, until our marriage in 1953. It continues today.

During the fall term of our junior year, close and mutual friends schemed to get us together. I was working at the "Y" (the Cadillac Youth Recreation Association) when a "going steady" couple, Jack Quinn, from my end of town, and Betty Brooks, who lived near Pat, and my friend, Dick Anderson, figured that Pat and I should get together. Loraine Henwood, Mary Bourassa, and others may have been party to the plot to have us become a couple. While I cannot recall our first official date, it was probably a dance at the Y or a movie at the Lyric Theater.

Memories of those happy days together included both the junior and senior year proms, post football game dances at the Y, picnics at the river, skiing, swimming at Community Beach, parties in friends' homes, soda fountains at Wooley's and Sigafooses', canoe trips, and other activities, almost always with a group of friends.

Those years might be considered as storybook. During that wartime period, true patriotism was rampant. Not surprisingly, war brought out the best in the people of Cadillac and elsewhere. Crime was almost non-existent (our homes and cars were never locked) and drinking among teenagers was rare.

Kindness prevailed among young and elderly alike. If not for the constant reminders of war with the mounting casualties and the strict rationing of goods, the setting would have been described as idyllic in every sense.

Pat was among the most popular students at Cadillac High School. She served as a class officer, member of the band, and, participated in theater productions. She was a very good student. Those activities along with her sensitive nature and pleasant personality made her a favorite among teachers and other adults, as well as her classmates. When I began dating Pat Chick, my parents seemed to feel increasingly satisfied about my ability to make good choices. The numbers "804," Pat's address on Farrar Street, and "431," her telephone number, remain embedded in my mind to this day.

After graduation in 1946, I enrolled at Central Michigan College of Education at Mt. Pleasant while Pat continued working at the Cadillac Evening News. We dated occasionally during my first two years in college.

I joined the US Navy in September 1948. Pat enrolled at Michigan State Normal College (Eastern Michigan) at Ypsilanti and after one year transferred to Central Michigan College. We continued our dating relationship when my home leaves from the Navy coincided with her trips back to Cadillac.

At Central Michigan Pat was elected to the Queen's Court at an October Homecoming event. She was a member of the Alpha Sigma Alpha sorority. She graduated from Central Michigan with her Bachelor Degree in Elementary Education.

Upon my discharge in September 1952, I re-enrolled at Central Michigan. Pat was teaching in the Lansing school system. We literally bumped into each other during Central's homecoming weekend at the "Bird," a student-gathering pub in Mt. Pleasant. Old feelings were rekindled and we returned to dating.

It was during the Christmas break in 1952 that I proposed to her. Of course, it was incumbent upon me to obtain the approval of her father before the final decision could be rendered. I suffered a degree of nervousness that exceeded the panic I experienced at a later occasion when I addressed 1,600 members of my national professional association. I survived the ordeal and received her father's endorsement for the matrimony. My parents, of course, were delighted!

Tradition dictated that the bride be the primary organizer of the wedding. Although teaching in another city, Pat planned a successful wedding event for June 20, 1953. The Reverend Edward Carlson, pastor of the Swedish Zion Lutheran Church, North Simon Street, Cadillac, administered the vows.

At the 2:00 PM ceremony, cousin Bob Peterson stood as my Best Man and Yvonne Peterson (no relation) as Pat's bridesmaid. A large number of guests filled the church, including Chick and Sjogren family members, most of my Delta Sigma Phi fraternity brothers from Central Michigan, a Navy friend, Joe Tierney from Boston, and many former classmates and friends from Cadillac and Lake City, Pat's home town. It was a ninety degree-day in Cadillac. The ceremony was conducted sans air conditioning.

Michigan Governor G. Mennen Williams was scheduled to be in Cadillac on that day so I sent him a wedding invitation. While his travel plans had changed, he sent a very thoughtful note wishing us well in our marriage.

The reception was held at the Cadillac Country Club on the shores of Lake Mitchell where we were serenaded by the fraternity guys and toasted by many.

Our post-wedding trip in my 1947 Oldsmobile coupe, the Blue Beetle, consisted of a drive north through Harbor Springs, Cross Village, and eventually to a motel in Mackinaw City. The following morning, it was a ferry trip across the straits and on to a delightful forest resort, Deer Track Village, about 50 miles northwest of Marquette. There followed a trip through Wisconsin to Palatine, Illinois, near Chicago, to visit Pat's sister, Colleen, and her family.

Without question, my life would have been far less satisfying had I not had the complete support and encouragement of Pat, my talented and beautiful wife of more than 63 years. While my activities achieved a financial condition that allowed us to enjoy travel and other life luxuries, her willingness to assume the majority of the parenting and home financial responsibilities contributed substantially to my ability to commit so much time for work and various professional activities.

Pat was the ideal mother for our children. Our parenting philosophies and practices seldom varied. Give children a long leash to test their level of maturity and tug it in a bit when their behaviors call for more control. Her influence on Steve, Jan, Sue, and Sig resulted in highly capable, family-oriented, caring folks who, with like-minded spouses, are now raising their children similarly.

Pat's handling of our finances gave our marriage a good balance, as I had no interest in the task. She studied the literature, attended classes, and talked to professionals about investments, insurance, and saving plans. As our net worth increased, Pat's insights into the issue became increasingly important.

Ours was not a simple life by any means. We occupied households in many places including a sublet MSU married student housing, trailer parks in Midland and Mt. Pleasant, a resort cabin on Crystal Lake near Frankfort, with my parents on South Mitchell Street and on Cass and Mason streets in Cadillac.

We lived in Ann Arbor while I attended the UM, three sites in Harbor Springs, Kalamazoo, two more sites in Ann Arbor, Pasadena, California, Long Lake in Traverse City, two sites on Mackinaw Trail in Cadillac, and finally a condo in downtown Cadillac. We also had properties in Hoxeyville and Wedgewood in Cadillac and The Villages in Florida. It wasn't that I could not hold a job; it was mostly moves where new opportunities awaited.

Pat and I agreed early on that because of my frequent travel our recreational activities would be those that could be enjoyed by the entire family. Thus, ski slopes and campgrounds became our primary destinations during vacations. I have not hunted deer or small game since the 1960's. I played on a U of M faculty softball team on occasion. I was a regular on the U of M racquetball and tennis courts, which were mostly hour-long contests.

Spring vacations saw us headed to the Colorado ski resorts numerous times and to Caberfae several weekends during the winter months. We camped in our trailer pop-up camper from the Yellowstone to Arizona, to across from Manhattan Island on the New Jersey Hudson River shore, and on the ski slopes in Vermont. Our family visited many campgrounds in both Michigan peninsulas.

Pat and I enjoyed many travel adventures together both before and after we became empty nesters. After "parking" the kids with their grandparents in Cadillac and Pat's sister, Colleen in Arizona, Pat accompanied me on an assignment to South America with visits to Columbia, Ecuador, and Peru where we stayed at Lima, Cuzco, and Machu Picchu. We also visited Hawaii, including stops in Kauai, Maui, and the "Big Island," following a two-week workshop on international education that I directed in Honolulu.

We took a memorable trip to Australia and New Zealand where we motored to many communities and met many residents of those remarkable countries. During several trips to Europe, with rental cars and a common interest in small hotels and B & B's, we explored Germany, France, Belgium, Switzerland, Italy,

Luxembourg, Austria, Czech Republic, Denmark, and Norway. On our two visits to Sweden, we were both able to research the history of our families, explore our ancestors' towns and villages, and meet with our Swedish relatives. Those were very special events for us.

As we approached our late 70's, we enjoyed several Caribbean and Alaskan cruises, a few Elderhostel's, extended wintertime stays in Southern Arizona, and trips to Colorado to be with our daughters, their families, and the ski slopes.

Each of our children is an independent thinker and possesses his and her own unique personality. All have worked in the trenches while in school and college and have since become very successful in their chosen professions. All eight of our children's children, Justin, Wes, Andrew, Jacob, Annie, Peter, Claire, and Will, excel in their academics as well as outside activities including music, athletics, and theatre.

My life has been greatly enriched by having Patricia Ruth Chick Sjogren at my side.

At my Grandmother's home site in Sweden. Seen in photo are Kenth Hansson, Swedish guide, brother Sig, his wife, Melissa, and Pat, c. 2008.

*Pat and author,
June 20, 1953*

*Pat and author,
c. 2004*

Family reunion (c. 2007) Crystal Mountain, Michigan

TEACHER, COACH, AND CAMP DIRECTOR

The mediocre teacher tells.
The good teacher explains.
The superior teacher demonstrates.
The great teacher inspires.
~ William Arthur Ward

Education is my profession. My introduction to educating others began as a swimming instructor at the Community Beach in Cadillac where I taught mostly elementary and pre-school children during the 1940's. After college, I taught high school students at Frankfort and Harbor Springs high schools and junior high students at Cadillac. Then it was Western Michigan University, The University of Michigan, and Southern California University where I adjusted my educational interests and became a university admissions officer.

FRANKFORT HIGH SCHOOL (1954 – 1955)

Panthers

My teaching career was launched during the fall of 1954 at Frankfort High School where I taught US and world history and government. Because of a staff resignation, I taught a girl's gym class during the second semester. I was also the head coach in football, basketball, and track. It was an ambitious assignment for a first-year teacher.

I thoroughly enjoyed teaching social studies as I attempted to pattern my instructional methods after my model, Mr. Sam Lee Nelson, my high school social studies teacher. My youthful sense of optimism served me well as I experimented successfully with new ways to motivate my students.

As a head coach, I experienced a "high" (football) and a "low," (basketball.) The only football game I lost was to a team that was coached by my back-up quarterback as a Cadillac Viking in 1945. I had introduced the new T-formation at Frankfort and George Telgenhoff, at Mesick High School, employed our old, but rather efficient offense at Cadillac, to defeat me 13 to 7.

In basketball, we were two and ten. Northport beat us 80 to 20 on their court. Our bus driver slipped out for a drink or two during the game and I had to drive the team bus back to Frankfort during a snowstorm on M-22, an unfamiliar winding rural road.

CADILLAC JUNIOR HIGH SCHOOL (1955 - 1957)

Vikings

After one year at Frankfort, I was recruited by Lynn Corwin, director of the Cadillac School Camp, to come to Cadillac to replace him as director of the camp. I was assigned to teach math and science at the Cadillac Junior High School and assist legendary CHS varsity football coach, Hi Becker, as the backfield coach, chief scout, and one year each as freshman and JV coach.

Teaching junior high students was a new learning experience for me, especially as I had never been trained to teach science and math courses at that level. It went well

Among my science teaching experiences was the unit on reptiles. I found a wire cage about four feet square in the school's attic. It soon became a cage for snakes, frogs, and turtles that I captured in area woods and displayed in the classroom for a few days.

I also remember releasing the critters back to nature. A pesky garter snake began making its way back to the road. As I reached to pick it up and return it to a safer area, it bit me on my hand. Maybe that's a snake's way of showing appreciation!

Coaching football at Cadillac was a very satisfying experience for me. My freshman team went undefeated, beating archrival Traverse City twice by wide margins. At the post game dinner at Dills restaurant in Traverse City, the owner praised the conduct and dress of my team suggesting that they were among the best-behaved squads they had served. Those athletes went on to provide coach Becker with an undefeated season and statewide recognition.

Two of our children were born during our short stay in Cadillac, Steve on April 23, 1956 and Jan, on September 3, 1957, only a few days before we departed for Ann Arbor. There I took advantage of a fellowship, an assistantship, and the G.I. Bill to complete a Master's Degree at The University of Michigan.

CADILLAC SCHOOL CAMP DIRECTOR

My Cadillac School Camp experiences in 1939, described in an earlier chapter, had a profound influence on my character and my professional and personal life. When Lynn Corwin, one of Cadillac's legendary educators and one who possessed an incredible human spirit, invited Pat and I to carry on the work so ably conducted for 16 years by Lynn and his wife, Marie, I accepted his offer.

It was the winter of 1955-56 and I was teaching at Frankfort High School. That winter Pat and I attended a Cadillac High School basketball home game. Before half time, Mr. Corwin, a man I respected and admired as much as anybody I have ever known, slid into the seat next to us and asked if I would like to direct the school camp.

With four years of college, four years of US Navy service, and one year of teaching, I felt at least somewhat qualified for such an assignment. While I don't remember Lynn's actual words, they went something like this; "If you like children and you like outdoor recreation and nature and you don't mind hard work, you can do the job." Of course, Lynn was too modest to add, "If you create the level of learning and fun experiences for the campers that have existed for the past nearly 16 years, it will make your job easier."

I accepted the position and we moved into the director's cabin as assistant director, while Lynn continued to serve that first year as director *in absentia*. The cook staff was retained and I hired Jack Bogner, a former Cadillac resident and camper and a teacher from Charlotte, as assistant director. Pat did the food buying and helped in camp crafts and other activities. In early June prior to the opening week, I borrowed my Dad's sprayer and painted the four original cabins. With the help of the school maintenance staff and Pat, we readied the camp for the mid-June launch.

In those days, we had eight weeks of camp; three weeks each of young boys and girls and one week each of older boys and girls. A bus picked up the campers at the six elementary schools each Sunday and returned them on Saturday mornings. We followed Lynn's schedule of activities. It was a very successful camping season. That June 1955 I changed the names and had signs made for all the cabins from numbers to the names of mostly Michigan Native American tribes.

The following year, my assistant director was Wendell Gabier, also a former camper, and brother of my good friend, Russ. The camp cook was Edward Babcock, my CHS chemistry and physics teacher during the mid-1940s. A challenge of the 1956 camp was caring for our baby in our small director's cabin that had no running water. Our first child, Steve, born two months earlier, was for the most part a camp "curiosity." While ignored by most of the boys, he was a big hit with the girls.

It was another successful camping year with few changes from Lynn's time-honored way of doing things at the school camp.

While I enjoyed working in my hometown, I could not resist the offer of both a fellowship and an assistantship from The University of Michigan. That decision led eventually to a career in college admissions. It was a good decision!

GRADUATE SCHOOL AT MICHIGAN (1957 / 1958)

Learning is a treasure that will follow its owner everywhere.
~ Chinese Proverb

While teaching in Cadillac in 1957, I enrolled in a University of Michigan extension course in Mesick. For some reason, the professor felt that I should enroll in a graduate program at the UM in Ann Arbor. I said, "Nope, not interested!" When I discussed the matter with Pat, she said, "Yes, let's do it!" She was pregnant with our second child and she thought better opportunities awaited us if I could earn another degree.

I thoroughly enjoyed teaching math and science to eighth graders and working with legendary CHS football coach, Hi Becker. Besides, skiing, fishing, and hunting were much better in northern Michigan than it would be in Ann Arbor. However, it was Pat's wish and I was becoming increasingly impressed with her wisdom when major family decisions had to be made.

My fellowship was in the physical education department and I was expected to teach golf as one of several courses an undergraduate student could elect to satisfy the physical education requirement. I knew nothing about golf, but found that the Women's Athletic department had a supply of skis, poles, and boots that I could borrow to teach Michigan's first ever course in Alpine (downhill) skiing. It was considered a successful year by the University, as I secured films, had equipment displays, and found that waxed skis slide rather well on the grass and snow mixture of Ann Arbor's Arboretum hills. We doubled up on weekly class periods towards the end of fall term to take advantage of winter snow. I was able to get my class members through stem turns which gave them confidence to travel north for some real skiing!

My assistantship consisted of managing the UM men's faculty intramural sports program. That may have been my most important educational experience at the U of M as I had to schedule several dozen men in a variety of intramural sports in a building with limited facilities. Learning to get along with faculty served me well during my later education and admissions position at Michigan

My educational interests were solidified that year. Counseling and international education would be my career choice.

My grades were considerably better than those at Central and my experience there was positive in all ways. I earned my Master of Science in Education degree in 1958.

HARBOR SPRINGS HIGH SCHOOL (1958 - 1960)

Rams

After earning my MA at the U of M, I returned to my beloved Northern Michigan. My third and final teaching position was at Harbor Springs, where I was the system-wide counselor and high school history teacher. I took the job primarily because a new ski slope, Nub's Nob, was to open and they needed a skier to assist with designing runs and to teach skiing on weekends. Pat suggested with justification that I took the position for the wrong reasons.

We enjoyed the community, the school, and nature's incredibly good work in that region. The teachers were a close-knit group and we found life filled with socials and numerous outdoor activities, including skiing, deer hunting, trout and lake fishing, and sailing in Little Traverse Bay. A highlight was the annual trout fishing weekend in Seney in the Upper Peninsula with the superintendent, principal, and several teachers.

A COLLEGE ADMISSION CAREER

The secret of success in life is for a man to be ready for his opportunity when it comes.
~ Benjamin Disraeli

Except for four years in the US Navy, four years at Central Michigan College, a summer in East Lansing, and a graduate school year in Ann Arbor, my early life was spent in northern Michigan. After living in and thoroughly enjoying Frankfort, Cadillac, and Harbor Springs, I was in no way attracted to a life elsewhere. As a ski patrolman and swimming instructor, I had met many downstate people who expressed their fond hopes of one day moving to the fresh air, green forests, inviting hills, and cool waters of northern Michigan. I felt sorry for them and expressed quiet thanks to my grandparents for finding their way from Sweden and Ontario to Cadillac in the late 1890's.

While I was thoroughly enjoying the outdoor life in northern Michigan and a rather stress free job as a teacher in Harbor Springs High School, Pat had other ideas. Sue Ann was born March 8, 1959 in Petoskey. With three children under the age of four, Pat was somewhat homebound while I was enjoying the slopes, streams, and forests. It was time for me to think more seriously about my role in my family's future.

WESTERN MICHIGAN UNIVERSITY (1960 - 1964)

Broncos
"Onward for the Brown and Gold!"

It all began in October 1959, at the Petoskey High School College Night. I was the guidance director and teacher at Harbor Springs High School. Russ Gabier, a good friend from Cadillac, representing Western Michigan University (WMU), casually asked if I might be interested in college admissions work. I said, "Not really. I like it up here." When I mentioned our conversation to Pat, she replied "Let's do it!" Pat mistakenly thought that if I landed a college position in southern Michigan, I would spend more time with her and our three children. She would also expect improved educational opportunities for our growing family as well as better professional possibilities for me. She was right!

The following spring, we were invited to Kalamazoo for the position interview. Several days later Pat received a call from WMU that I had been the chosen candidate for the position and that WMU wanted our decision as soon as possible. With a small group of school staff members, I had just departed on our annual Seney fishing trip. Pat immediately called the Mackinac Bridge authority in St. Ignace to deliver the important message to me at the tollbooth. Her request was politely denied. She called the Seney cabin owner to deliver the message to me. Knowing her strong desire to move to Kalamazoo, I told her I would accept it immediately.

Because there was no stationery supply store in Seney, I had to be creative. I wrote my acceptance to the WMU offer on the back of a Seney Bar cocktail napkin. It served the purpose and in early September 1960, I became an admissions counselor at WMU. (I assume that my acceptance document was quickly shredded!)

The college admissions field was a good fit for me. It offered frequent contact with a most interesting variety of people under an endless array of emotional circumstances. The position required self-confidence, a willingness to work long hours, and an ability to carry out some complicated and important responsibilities. It would also require much travel.

The profession provided me with the opportunity to test and stretch my abilities and to eventually travel the US and the world to undertake interesting and important assignments. I would confront a variety of challenges that strengthened my organizational and social skills. Happy in my newfound profession, I felt that I was one of the luckiest guys in the world.

As I progressed up the promotional ladder, I always seemed to have a strong support group, at home, in the workplace, and in the many professional organizations with which I was associated.

I enjoyed my four years at Western. An early decision by me would have a major impact on my career and my life. When I was ready to take on additional responsibilities, I was given the choice of managing either financial aid or foreign student admissions. I quickly opted for the latter. Mr. Sam Lee Nelson, my high school World History teacher, was once again the major influence for that decision.

That choice launched my role as one of a handful of college administrators throughout the country who accepted the task of examining foreign educational experiences to determine the quality standards and level comparability with US courses and school learning certificates. Through publications, workshops, and presentations at associational meetings we circulated to the admissions community the results of our research. The process also attracted countless dozens of admissions officers from throughout the US, Canada, and elsewhere, to engage in this rising professional challenge.

That initiative added a new dimension to my professional life. It led to many trips abroad and the presidency of a nationwide university admission organization (American Association of Collegiate Registrars and Admission Officers.) Through some hard work, a keen interest, and a bit of luck, I had become a major player in the process of creating and disseminating publications and presentations worldwide on the proper assessment of international education credentials that facilitated the transfer of students and scholars between nations.

My responsibilities at WMU included interviewing prospective applicants to the University both on campus and on the road throughout Michigan and northern Indiana and Illinois. At College Nights, I would sometimes address groups of 100, or more, and at other times a family, or two. It was a demanding, but highly satisfying job.

A typical October week might have me departing early Monday morning for a Midland school visit from where I would leave for a series of school visits in Pinconning and Tawas City. After dinner in Alpena, with some college admission officers, I would represent the university at a College Night at the local high school. There I would give three 30-minute presentations about WMU.

On Tuesday, after a similar pattern of school visits during the day, I would arrive for a College Night in Petoskey. Wednesday, it was on to Traverse City and finally to Cadillac on Thursday. While I always enjoyed the Thursday dinner with Mom and Dad at home, I usually had to explain why I looked so tired!

During my third year at WMU, I took on financial aid as well. That assignment consisted of awarding State of Michigan Board scholarships to several hundred entering freshmen.

All my assignments at WMU proved to be both interesting and challenging, especially school visits and interviewing prospective candidates for admission. Russ Gabier, director of admissions and Clayton Maus, registrar, were men of high standards of professionalism and always insisted that when making decisions, the students' interests were to be paramount. They were good mentors for me during my introduction to a college admissions career.

Pat was satisfied with the move to Kalamazoo even though my job responsibilities kept me away from home many nights. We lived in a very nice neighborhood and the WMU staff welcomed us with open arms. The children could walk to a modern elementary school and had many playmates.

Our fourth child, Sigurd, was born on December 18, 1962 in Kalamazoo and at a very early age charmed the many pre-school friends of his brother and two sisters. We made frequent visits to Cadillac for recreation and family affairs. Summer vacations were typically spent camping, highlighted by a lengthy trip to Arizona when our youngest was but four months old. We found that Kalamazoo was as satisfying as northern Michigan as a place to raise our family.

While our departure from Kalamazoo was difficult, the life experiences that followed eased the pain.

THE UNIVERSITY OF MICHIGAN (1964 - 1988)

Wolverines
"Go Blue!"
"Hail to the Victors!"

After rejecting an admissions staff position offer from The University of Michigan in 1963, I succumbed to the second UM offer and we moved to Ann Arbor in fall 1964 where we experienced 24 years of a very satisfying professional and personal life. Pat and the children enjoyed their new home community immensely by taking advantage of the countless educational, social and recreational activities the Ann Arbor community provided.

The University of Michigan hired me as assistant director of admissions with the primary responsibility of providing services to high schools. I was encouraged to begin working on my doctorate. Clyde Vroman, director of admissions and his very able associate director, Gayle Wilson, made sure that I had time available in my busy schedule to enroll in classes.

Because my primary responsibility when hired was to strengthen the relationship between the University and secondary schools in Michigan and elsewhere, setting aside time for coursework was a challenge. Much travel was required. Further, four children at home deserved my time and attention.

By 1972, I had completed the required coursework, passed all preliminary examinations, had my doctoral thesis proposal accepted after which I wrote and defended my paper. It led to my PhD in International Education. My thesis was entitled "Foreign Students in Michigan Community and Junior Colleges: An Analysis of Present Conditions, Experiences, and Expectations."

During my first year at the UM, I scheduled myself for 100 high school visits, all in Michigan. While I talked to counselors and students about the university, I spent much of my time listening to the concerns of those who I was assigned to serve. It was a real eye-opener for me and for our office. Counselors were critical of some of U of M's policies and procedures, but highly appreciative that someone from the university would seek their opinions on what needed to be done. Vroman and Wilson provided me with work flexibility to improve our relationships and services to our important constituencies; high school counselors, students, and their parents. The changes made during my first few years in Ann Arbor would form the basis for the policies and processes that would guide undergraduate admissions for years to come.

We did not use such terms as "recruiting" and "marketing" in those days. Many saw the University as an elitist institution, particularly those populations from low income, rural, inner city, and northern and western Michigan counties. With the onset of the post-war "Baby Boom" (children born soon after World War II,) a new strategy needed to be put into place to handle the yearly double-digit increases of high school graduates of the mid and late 1960s. Working with Vroman and Wilson, who George Hanford, the College Board president, claimed were the "best one-two punch in college admissions," I developed skills that would serve me well throughout my career.

In 1972, Vroman was on an extended government financed assignment in Japan. He was expected to retire soon after his return and Wilson was the heir apparent to the directorship. Regrettably, Wilson died unexpectedly during Vroman's absence. Lance Erickson and I were left to manage things. We became a two-person directorship. Lance was responsible for internal operations and I handled external affairs. It worked well.

The University embarked on a national search for Vroman's replacement and Lance, a dear friend, and I were candidates. In 1973, after nine years as assistant director, I was appointed director of undergraduate admissions at the university.

I was deeply honored and somewhat humbled to be awarded such an important position in one of America's premier universities. I was to hold that position until 1988, the year of my UM retirement. I appointed Lance as my executive associate director and began the process of reorganizing an experienced staff of about 45 clerical and professional workers.

Soon after my appointment in 1973, I undertook an assignment that included a weekend hiatus in Stockholm, Sweden. I found a sidewalk café in Old Stockholm where I sat for several hours over a two-day period drinking coffee, eating breads, fish and cheese, finger foods, and writing a complete operational plan for the University of Michigan Admissions Office! Grandpa Frans Sjogren would have been proud!

While in Sweden, I penned an adage that would be shared with those I managed. It would represent my approach to my work life and it displayed for the staff my hopes and expectations about their work performances. That adage was "Work hard, work smart, and have fun doing it." Most of the hundreds of professional and support staff members under my watch embraced the concept. My staffs at both the University of Michigan and the University of Southern California were ones with exceptionally small job attrition rates.

The early 1970's was a difficult period for the University. The Black Action Movement was well entrenched and making some impossible demands on the UM's admission policies. My Native American admissions officer led a "sit-in" in my office! Under President Robben Fleming's good leadership, the UM escaped some of the major difficulties experienced by other prestigious institutions.

My management style was highly influenced by the freedom and mature treatment I received by my parents as a "child of the great depression." The door to my office was always open. I frequently circulated among the professional and support staffs asking questions and delivering praise where warranted. Never was a staff member criticized in general office or public open areas. All were encouraged to find ways to do their work more efficiently and to find and suggest ways of improving office operations. All of my senior staff members were requested to embrace a staff management process that was similar to my management style.

That approach seemed to work well in Ann Arbor. When I took over, nearly all of the professional staff members were men with northern European surnames. I immediately began recruiting women and minorities to fill vacancies. Friends in other institutions were impressed with the exceptionally low employee attrition of our office. I had control over salaries and rewarded those who performed well, a strategy that encouraged all to perform up to their abilities. There was an unusually good distribution of skills among the professional staff.

I was frequently asked to voice opinions on minority student admission issues with faculties and senior University administrators. My suggestions were seriously considered. I suggested "targets" rather than the common term, "quotas." Most importantly, I convinced senior administrators that admission standards for black students had to be brought more in line with traditional freshman standards as the severe attrition rate of minorities was causing us problems recruiting in Detroit and other urban schools. I spent a good deal of my time defending UM's admission practices to citizen's groups, Rotary Clubs, and various elements of the University community.

The challenge was to meet the new enrollment targets with well-qualified students in each of the nine academic schools and colleges to which freshmen were considered. Further, each unit had in-state and non-resident targets. Sub groups, such as minorities, alumni sons and daughters, faculty families, athletes, special talent candidates, veterans, returning women whose education may have been interrupted while raising a family, and others expected and received special consideration, although not by reducing the admission standards.

I developed a unique process of projecting for each of UM's schools and colleges and the numerous sub groups, the numbers of applications, admission offers needed, and student acceptances predicted to meet the enrollment targets. We seldom missed by more than two or three percent.

Our relationships with the academic units, as well as the president's office, fund-raising staff, deans, and various student groups remained strong and positive during my tenure at the UM.

While my most challenging responsibility was with the head coaches of major sports, it was not a hostile environment. Don Canham, director of athletics at that time was very supportive of the admissions office and his coaches were to treat us with respect and consideration. They did so! Canham was the largest contributor to my U of M retirement gift.

The coaches at Michigan frequently voiced their frustration over our high admissions policies and for good reason. During my 24 years at the University (1964 -1988) the most rigorous Big Ten admission standards were those of Northwestern University and The University of Michigan. Many if not most of the premier recruits who did not meet the admissions standards of those two institutions would later be seen on the fields, courts, and ice arenas competing against the U of M. A few Big Ten schools by state mandates were required to admit all residents who graduated from an instate accredited high school.

    We had an advantage, as well. Thanks to Don Canham's masterful ability to promote UM athletics, we usually led the conference in football ticket sales. With that income, academically marginal athletes could expect well-managed support services. Legendary UM football coach Bo Schembechler would occasionally visit with me to show the success rates of some of the questionable admits. Those data were impressive. During my tenure as director not more than a dozen borderline admits (by my definition) failed to complete U of M degree requirements. Of course, some returned to college after years on professional teams. Interestingly, I sometimes see those "failures" on televised sports announcing intercollegiate contests as intelligent and articulate broadcasters.

    I suspect that most great athletes possess above average intelligence, discipline, organizational skills, and other assets or they would not have achieved such lofty performance levels.

    Michigan was a good fit for me. As its director of admissions, I had numerous opportunities to participate in national and worldwide professional activities. I assumed leadership roles in many of them. My student-centered philosophy and staff management skills have guided others in the profession to avoid the all-to-common "admit by machine" strategy, or what I call a "very efficient way to do the wrong thing."

    I shall forever be thankful to The University of Michigan for giving me the flexibility to stretch my creativeness and management abilities. It was a great ride! Upon retirement, however, the only question was, "Which northern Michigan community will it be?"

UNIVERSITY OF SOUTHERN CALIFORNIA (1989 - 1993)

Trojans
"Fight On for ol' SC"

During the late 1980's, I joined a small group of the country's leading admission directors on a team consultation at the University of Southern California in downtown Los Angeles. Being a private inner city costly institution with some serious public relations problems, as well as competing for students with arguably the best public university system in the US, the decision was made to bring in consultants.

The USC admission and financial aid operations were in turmoil as mostly inexperienced people had been hired to fill the important position.

A few months after the consultation the USC President James Zumberge, a former UM professor and friend of UM president Robben Fleming, directed his provost to recruit me as the USC dean of admissions and financial aid. After a few refusals, I finally accepted under the condition that I could spend several weeks during the summers in Michigan. It was soon after my retirement from The University of Michigan in 1988 that we had settled into our Traverse City lakeside home. I was now the dean of admissions and financial aid at one of the best private universities in the country. I had a staff of 150 professionals and support workers.

I chose to work without a contract so that I could fix a broken process without concern of being retained if they disapproved of my work. I knew that serious changes would be necessary and in that environment many staff members might not be supportive. At that time, Pat and I were confident that we could live on our

U of M retirement so the USC position was not terribly important.

My first task was to set up a comprehensive communication plan to keep administration, staff, and the community advised monthly of the issues, our progress, and the results. I personally visited dozens of the best high schools in southern California to advise them of the University's new look. Immediately, we increased both the number of applications and the quality of the entering freshman class. I was also able to save the University over $500,000 the first year mostly by redesigning publications and greatly reducing application processing and mail costs.

While in California Pat and I traveled to many interesting sites from our home in Pasadena, including museums, historical and natural sites, and theatre presentations. Every summer we returned to our home on Long Lake in Traverse City although I would return to the office two or three times during the summer to handle management issues.

The Provost had asked me to serve for at least five years. I responded that I would remain for three years unless more time was needed to fix things. I hired an excellent director of admissions and a financial aid director and departed after four years with many expressions of appreciation from the administrative staff and faculty.

After a successful four-years in sunny California we moved back to our Traverse City home on Long Lake. We left Los Angeles pleased with our accomplishments at the University and feeling much better about our financial future.

*Author's childhood home at 723 Wood Street
(South Mitchell) c.1922
Rye and Lib Gould Children (Ward, Elgie, Pauline,
Pearl, Morley)*

*First retirement home at
1027 South Long Lake Rd.
Traverse City, Mich. (1988 – 2001)*

Author's Home,
305 East Mason St.,
Cadillac, Mich.
(Years 1955 – 1957)

Second Retirement Home
7774 Mackinaw Trail
Cadillac, Mich. (2001-2014)

Author's Home, 2885 Renfrew Street,
Ann Arbor, Mich. (1964 – 1988)

INTERNATIONAL TRAVEL

The world is a book, and those who do not travel read only a page.
~ St. Augustine

While serving as director of admissions at The University of Michigan, I was frequently called upon to assume overseas assignments, ranging from a few days to three or four weeks.

The nature of these visits ranged from providing college admission, college life, and financial aid information to Americans and non-Americans in US overseas schools; leading and participating in country or region-specific educational credential workshops; examining and writing about country educational systems; creating degree and certificate equivalencies between the US and other countries; advising foreign students and counselors on college admission in the US; and selecting students for placement in prestigious US universities.

Sponsors for these trips included the US Department of State Office of Overseas Schools (AOS), the College Board, the US Bureau of Education and Cultural Affairs, the Fulbright Commission, Youth for Understanding (Norway) the German/American Academic Exchange Program, Michigan Partners of the Americas (Belize,) the US Department of Defense Office of Dependent Schools (DODDS,) the AACRAO / NAFSA Joint Committee on Workshops, the Nordic Council (Denmark, Finland, Iceland, Norway, Sweden,) the African Scholarship Program of American Universities (ASPAU) and its companion group for Latin America (LASPAU), presenter at the prestigious Council of University Administrators of the United Kingdom, International Baccalaureate Programme (IB), UNESCO, and a dozen consulting visits to the *Universidad Autonoma de Mexico in Pueblo, Mexico.*

The American Schools in Athens and Tel Aviv sponsored me on a consulting trip to those Eastern Mediterranean Sea communities. Several self-sponsored trips with my wife, Pat, to Europe and the Caribbean Sea countries were also made. At USC I travelled to six East Asian countries on a private Gulfstream IV aircraft with six colleagues from the University to host alumni receptions and recruiting visits at international schools.

Most of the trips were tightly scheduled. A typical day consisted of arising at 4:30 AM, a two or three-hour flight, a full day in the school, meetings with school boards and US Embassy staffs, and a college night for students, parents and embassy staffs with retirement to a hotel or host US family at 11:00 PM.

The travel and school visits left me with both pleasant and a few with rather less than pleasant memories. They included 1951 ski trips in the Alps while serving in the US Navy, flying with a drunken bush pilot in southern Africa, a dose of tear gas in Peru, hassles by Jordanian security officers in Amman, confrontation with a huge rat in my hotel in Managua, dining on dog, tongue, ducks' feet, etc., in Taipei, skiing in Iran, and returning to Ann Arbor from Lahore, Pakistan with my luggage and two rather large Middle East tribal rugs.

Appendix Two includes a list of the countries and political subdivisions I have visited, including those while serving in the US Navy (1948 – 1952) and vacation trips with Pat. In all, I visited over 100 countries, some several times. All visits except those to Angola, Macao, Togo and Guam included at least one overnight stay and I did not include stops in which I remained on the plane or in the airport.

Friends in the profession have often remarked that I have probably had more non-university sponsored overseas assignments than any other admission officer. They were probably right! Fortunately, the University of Michigan and the

University of Southern California supported my participation in my 35 to 40 overseas assignments that took place between 1964 and 1993.

I was raised in a family that did not judge people by their color, their economic status, nor their religion. The "n" word was never voiced at family gatherings. Dad reminded me to treat everybody as an equal and that one should be judged as an individual and not as a member of a particular group classification. His words stayed with me as I traveled the world. I was comfortable in Pakistan, Iran, Venezuela, Botswana, and other places because most people in those places, I found, shared a value system much like mine. Of the many places I have visited, never have I felt an urgency to leave because of an unfriendly treatment.

PROFESSIONAL ORGANIZATIONS

I never worry about action, only inaction.
~ Sir Winston Churchill

I was a member and a leader of a number of national professional organizations. Those of which I am most proud include service as both President and Vice President for International Education of the American Association of Collegiate Registrars and Admission Officers (AACRAO); a twenty-six year Board of Directors member of the International Baccalaureate of North America (IBNA); founding member and chair of the Admission Section, National Association for Foreign Student Affairs (NAFSA); chair, International Education Committee of the College Board (CB,) and two major leadership position in the National Collegiate Athletic Association (NCAA.) (Please see my *Vita* in Appendix Six for a complete list of organizations and leadership positions held.)

American Association of College Admission Officers and Registrars (AACRAO) 1962 – Life. AACRAO was my primary professional organization. After holding a number of committee chairs, I was elected Vice President for International Education for a three-year term in the late 1970's. At the Annual Meeting in San Francisco, I was elected president of the association to serve during the 1981-1982 year. I was awarded AACRAO's highest honors, the Distinguished Service Award, the Award for Excellence in International Education, and Honorary and Life Membership.

In 1996, while retired, I was asked to manage the Washington D.C. office for

AACRAO President (1981 – 1982)

several weeks when the executive director at that time was dismissed. My major task was to downsize both office space and staff and lead the effort to recruit a new executive director. My assignment was completed successfully and the new hire remained in his position for many years

College Board: (1969 to retirement) As the official University of Michigan (and subsequently USC) representative, I attended nearly every national and regional meeting of the College Board for 20 years. I served as chair of the International Education

Committee and held other committee positions. As a College Board user, I testified before a congressional committee on proposed testing legislation. Our side won!

International Baccalaureate Organization (IBO) (North American Region, 1969 to c. 2009) I served on the North American Board from 1974 until 2001, the most years ever served by a Board member. I wrote position papers, crafted policies and procedures, led teams throughout North America and the Caribbean for onsite school certification into the IB, monitored examinations, and carried out a number of other tasks.

I am particularly pleased that I assisted my daughter Sue with her leadership in establishing the IB at ThunderRidge (not a typo) High School in Colorado where her children were enrolled. Sue and Stephen's children, Annie and Peter, graduated with IB diplomas from the school. A third grandchild, Nancy and Sig's daughter, Claire, earned her IB diploma at Walled Lake Western High School in Michigan.

National Association for Foreign Student Affairs (NAFSA) (1962 – Life Membership awarded). I helped create and presented to the NAFSA Board a proposal to sponsor an Admission Section in the Association and served as one of its early chairs. I also designed and directed the first overseas workshop on foreign student admissions in Hawaii and a second one on the five Nordic Countries in Norway. I served on several committees and turned down an invitation to be considered for the organization's president.

National Collegiate Athletic Association (1977 to 1988) I testified before a judge in Washington DC as an expert witness in support of the NCAA on a foreign student eligibility case. Our side won!

I also drafted the highly controversial Proposition #48 that strengthened freshman academic requirements for university student athletes. After lengthy debate, the proposal, somewhat amended, was approved by the NCAA membership. Prop #48 called for students to complete courses in specified academic areas and present a satisfactory test score. It replaced a rule that merely called for a 2:00 grade point average in all coursework. I also drafted and proposed changes in the satisfactory progress rule.

I was a member of and chaired the Academic Requirements Committee of NCAA. I created and chaired for 20 years the NCAA Foreign Student Credential Evaluation Committee that wrote and published institutional freshmen and transfer student guidelines to determine the academic requirements for foreign student athletes seeking participation in varsity sports in US colleges and universities.

Overseas School Project (OSP- 1972 – 1996) I was one of five admission professionals who provided guidance to overseas Americans in schools throughout the world. After four years visiting East Asia schools, Hong Kong, Manila, Seoul, Bangkok, Singapore, Tokyo, Jakarta, Kuala Lumpur, and Taipei, I was assigned Central America and the Caribbean.

I was then assigned to the Middle East, configured to include schools from Rabat, Barcelona, and Madrid on the West to Kathmandu and Dhaka on the East. Major stops also included Cairo, Athens, Tel Aviv, Amman, Kuwait City, Islamabad, Lahore, Karachi, Colombo, New Delhi, Sri Lanka, and Bombay (now Mumbai.) Typical schools enrolled 20% to 30% Americans, and the rest from as many as 25 or more countries. Usually only two days were spent in a visited city.

Test of English as a Foreign Language (TOEFL)– During the early 1970's I served for three years as committee chair. In 2005 to 2008 I was again appointed as a member. I was offered and declined the position as director of the program in the 1960's. TOEFL is an Educational Testing Service program based in Princeton, NJ.

US Department of Defense Dependent Schools. (DODDS 1980-1987) I met with counselors, students, and parents in overseas DODD schools to provide advice on college entrance in the US. Those assignments took me to Army, Navy, and Air Force bases in Japan, Italy, Holland, Germany, Korea, and Spain.

SELECTED PUBLICATIONS AUTHORED

My career in college admissions consisted of more than reading applications. I wrote two books, several major manuscripts, and many articles for professional journals. A few of which I am most proud are:

A) *Diversity, Accessibility, Quality – A Brief introduction to American Education for Non-Americans.* (College Board, 1977 –second edition, 1986.) Translated into several foreign languages and distributed worldwide.

B) *Norway – A guide to the Admission and Academic Placement of Norwegian Students in North American Colleges and Universities.* (College Board, 1985) Co-authored with Lornie Kerr, Northwestern Michigan College. For our work I was honored at a 1988 reception hosted in the Norwegian Embassy, Wash. D.C. by Kjell Eliasson, Norwegian Ambassador to the United States. I was presented with *SNORRI: The Sagas of Viking Kings of Norway*, a magnificent 685 - page leather bound book that included the Ambassador's thoughtful handwritten personal statement.

C) *College Admissions and the Transition to Postsecondary Education: Standards and Practices.* Primary college admissions paper for President Reagan's initiative, *A Nation at Risk: The Imperative for Educational Reform.* (1983, The National Commission on Excellence in Education.) The report has been printed both in an AACRAO Monograph Series (No. 42, April 1989, 26 pp.) and the February 1983 issue of the National Association of Secondary School Principals, *NASSP Bulletin*.

D) Wrote original draft of NCAA proposal #48. (Substantially increased course and test of requirements of student-athletes to satisfy freshman eligibility rules. Presented to the NCAA Presidents Council by University of Michigan President Harold Shapiro. Approved and implemented with some modifications.)

MEMORABLE ADVENTURES

If you reject the food, ignore the customs, fear the religion, and avoid the people, you might better stay home.
~ James Michener

At a very early age Western themed movies and action literature about exciting Africa and mysterious Asia embedded in me a sense of adventure. I owe that enthusiasm for world travel to my favorite Cadillac High School teacher, Sam Lee Nelson and one of my favorite authors, Jack London, Thus, when opportunities to combine my professional abilities with overseas travel assignments came drifting my way, particularly those in Third World countries, I seldom refused the invitation to serve. (All travel assignment expenses abroad were paid by the sponsoring organization, mostly by US government agencies.)

Thank you Mr. London and Mr. Nelson!

Following are but a few of the many unusual experiences I had mostly overseas as a sailor and an educational consultant.

MURDER IN KEY WEST (1949)

While on shore patrol duty on a small cay between the Boca Chica Naval Air Station and Key West, my partner and I parked our jeep at a tavern for a late-night hamburger and coffee. At one end of the U-shaped bar sat a chief petty officer and at the other, a petite woman who owned the bar. We were in the middle.

Soon, a very obese man entered and approached the woman uttering the words, "This is it!" In an instant, the woman swung her stool to face the man head on and fired seven shots into the middle parts of his body. As she moved quickly to the kitchen, the chief, my friend and I made our way to the severely injured man lying face up on the floor.

As we stood contemplating our next move, the woman returned with a new clip in her 7mm pistol, stood over the man, and deposited two more bullets into his throat. As the man lie gasping his final breaths, his left arm fell across my foot. The chief grabbed the gun from the woman who then quietly lit a cigarette and sat at the bar stool with a broad smile on her face awaiting the police.

As an eyewitness to this high profile murder, I was called on for my testimony several times over the ensuing weeks during the cross-examination. Because there had been a warrant to keep the victim from the vicinity of the woman's workplace, the jury concluded that it was a "justifiable homicide" and she was set free, even though she had returned to finish the slaying of the completely immobile man.

THE GUNS OF ZAMBOANGA (1965)

In July 1965, I was awarded a six week Fulbright consultant grant to visit several Philippine high schools and universities to discuss educational opportunities for advanced study in US universities. After visiting Manila and other institutions in Luzon, my travel partner and I separated to travel solo in the sprawling areas of the Mindanao and Visayas island groups of the south. A memorable experience occurred in Zamboanga, Mindanao, a large city located in the extreme southwest tip of Mindanao.

At that time, a growing population of militant Muslims was fighting for independence from the Philippines. My assignment consisted of a visit to a university in a Muslim-dominated section of the city.

After the late afternoon meetings, I was one of two guests of honor to be recognized at a social hour and dinner, where guests were seated on the floor to hear a series of political speeches. It was election time in the Philippines and the natives there take their politics very seriously. Generally, the sides were divided along pro and anti-Americanism. I had earlier witnessed in Manila a mob stoning the American embassy.

To assist me through the evening program, I was provided with two teenaged English-speaking girls to keep me advised of the various protocols of eating, applauding, and general social conduct. As we sat on the long narrow hall floor, various speakers in their native language, Tagalog, discussed current political issues with frequent references to my country. It became rather uncomfortable for me as a number of times, most eyes in the assembly were directed towards me to observe my reaction to some anti-American tirade. I could not understand what was said.

Noting that smoking was permitted, I reached in my suit coat pocket to remove my pipe. Suddenly, several of the guards trained their rifles on me. The hall became silent except for the clicks of rifle safeties being released. The speaker stopped his speech and glared intently in my direction without a hint of a smile. One of my attendants quickly clasped my hand holding the pipe and slowly elevated it so all could see my "weapon." My embarrassed smile was met first with serious stares followed by sighs of relief that bullets flying about the hall were prevented by a quick-thinking young girl.

At the reception following the talks, many dinner attendees, including the speaker, offered apologies. I learned a lesson: never reach in your pockets for an item that could be mistaken for a gun during a speech given in a language other than my own!

FLIGHT OVER THE KALAHARI (1966)

For a number of reasons, a visit through several southern African countries under the African Scholarship Program of American Universities (ASPAU) program was one of my most memorable. I was a member of a two-person team assigned to visit Kenya and Tanzania to select young Africans for placement in 20 of America's most prestigious universities, including The University of Michigan.

My assignment companion and good friend was the Executive Director of the United Negro College Fund. While interviewing in Dar es Salaam and Nairobi, we were asked by the Boston office of ASPAU to extend our assignment for "serious political reasons." My colleague was to visit the Seychelles, an island in the Indian Ocean, and I was to conduct selection interviews in Bechuanaland (now Botswana) and Swaziland.

The next several days proved to be a bit more than simply "interesting." The native populations at many African countries during the 1960's were demanding independence from European colonizers, a movement known in the Swahili language as "Uhuru," or "Free Africa." The two countries assigned to me had recently achieved independence. Visits to those countries would require travel to Rhodesia, now Zimbabwe, which continued under European rule. Being Caucasian, I had a better chance than my African - American partner of securing the necessary travel documents for entry into several countries to complete my assignment.

To get to Lobatse, Bechuanaland, I had to fly to Blantyre, Malawi from Nairobi where I would connect on a flight to Salisbury, Rhodesia (now Harare, Zimbabwe.) There, I would take a train to Bulawayo in

Southern Rhodesia. A US Embassy-arranged charter flight would take me to Lobatse.

Because of a flight delay, a frequent occurrence in Africa, I was forced to spend a night in Blantyre, where, because of a shortage of lodging, I shared a room with a German and an Italian. Both were World War II veterans and we enjoyed an evening of conversation about the "war to end all wars." They displayed a genuine respect and admiration for the US military and Americans in general.

The following morning, I flew from Blantyre to Salisbury, Rhodesia. Under the leadership of Ian Smith, Rhodesia, a British Protectorate, refused to capitulate to black African demands that the government be turned over to the indigenous population. Severe restrictions on Rhodesian commerce, including trade embargos that were applied by Britain, US and most European nations failed to deter Smith's arrogant stand against the inevitable "Uhuru" movement.

Although world opinion, including, Britain itself, turned against the renegade regime, Ian Smith refused to budge. Because neighboring Bechuanaland, a former British High Commission Territory, had recently been granted African rule, Rhodesian authorities were reluctant to allow my passage to that territory. I presume that they thought I was reporter / writer cruising the area to obtain political stories from the local populations.

As a safeguard, I visited the Union of South Africa consulate in Salisbury and, after much convincing and a bit of stretching the truth about my reasons for wanting to visit South Africa, I secured a visa, which might be needed to facilitate my travel to and from Bechuanaland. Neither the Rhodesian nor Union of South African whites were eager to have black populations educated, particularly in America. Thus, my visits were somewhat clandestine. The reasons I gave for travel: Tourism and to study the education systems of British East and South Africa. It worked!

Interestingly, mistaken for a local resident in Salisbury, I was approached for a sidewalk TV interview to respond to the question: "What do you think of the world's trade embargo on Rhodesian tobacco." Another question asked what "Tellie" shows do I watch. Suspicion arose when I answered "Gun Smoke" and "I Love Lucy." It was near the end of my response when the young lady finally realized that I was an American. I doubt very much that they ran that clip on the Salisbury evening news show.

That evening, I took the train to Bulawayo, Rhodesia. The following morning, I taxied to the small airport to secure my charter flight to Lobatse, some 600 miles south of Bulawayo. The plane was a very old and very small single engine Cessna and the pilot was a rather old, ruddy, and a somewhat nasty drunk! During the early morning taxi to our takeoff position, he reached for what I hoped was water. I soon learned that it was not! Alas, his first swig was from his stashed bottle of whiskey.

After we were airborne, he said as he patted his chest, "I've got a bad ticker here, "Matey" and, while offering me "a snort," which I politely refused, he told me what to do if he had a heart attack while in flight. Because of the airplane noise and his thick Rhodesian brogue, I understood very little of what he had to say. I had visions of various Kalahari Desert carnivores fighting over my splattered body on the rocks and sand some 5,000 feet below us.

After several more snorts and one of the scariest landings of my life, we arrived safely. I immediately advised the man to take his plane and go home without me. Of course, he said that he possessed my only possible transportation out of Lobatse, but I didn't care. Better that I become a permanent Kalahari resident than die. He shrugged his shoulders, took another drink, and wished me good luck as he returned to his Cessna.

Lobatse is a seedy town near the Union of South Africa border. I was lodged in the town's best hotel (shared bath, no air conditioning, no TV). I soon met my ASPAU contact, Mrs. Pauline Chieppi, for dinner on the hotel porch. She was a member of a distinguished native African family who worked feverishly to assist young Africans in obtaining higher education abroad. She informed me that we would have to wait for two days to bring the students to the desert village about 30 kilometers from Lobatse.

Mrs. Chieppi advised me that the reason for my visit was due to the previous ASPAU team's failure to carry out their assignment in Bechuanaland. She did not want to chance another disappointment for her students.

When she departed, the hotel manager advised me, "Even though Bechuanaland was taken from us whites, we don't associate with the coloreds, especially on the porch of this hotel." It was a stern warning that I refused to heed.

Early Monday morning, Mrs. Chieppi drove me to the chieftain's grass and mud hut in the Kalahari where I was treated like royalty as the breakfast guest of the village elders. With my African colleagues, I interviewed about eight students, all of whom I could recommend for a US college placement.

Following the successful assignment, I had to find alternative transportation out of town. A train running from Johannesburg, Union of South Africa to Bulawayo was to stop in Lobatse the next morning. South Africa retained diplomatic relations with Ian Smith and was a strong supporter of Rhodesia.

When I boarded the train, I was momentarily flabbergasted. I was given a very comfortable "sleeper suite" next to the dining car and as far as I could determine, I was the train's only fare. When I enquired about the lack of passengers, the dining car's single staff member advised me that, because this train provides Ian Smith with his only source of supplies, several acts of sabotage and some terrorist's incidents had transpired along the tracks in recent weeks. As was true with the trip down, it was not a relaxing trip back. I experienced my only "white knuckle" train ride!

I made it through okay. It was indeed an interesting 20-hour voyage through the Kalahari Desert and several Bushman villages and a journey-long conversation with a personable African dining car attendant.

From Bulawayo, I flew to Lorenzo Marques (now named Maputo), Mozambique to secure another charter hop, this time to Mbabane, Swaziland. My plane first landed in Beira in Northern Mozambique where, upon looking out my window, I observed my bag being taken away by an airport official. I hopped down from the plane (no passenger regulations here!) and proceeded to ask why my bags were removed while other passengers escaped the procedure. I was told repeatedly but without reason that my bag could not be released from customs.

After about 20 minutes of haggling during which the plane was at ready for departure, I realized that some "dash" (African bribe) might be called for. A friend had had a similar experience in West Africa so I figured that it might work here. If it didn't work, my next experience might have been in a Mozambique jail. It did work, and after the $3.40 investment in my future, I climbed back aboard and with the other smiling passengers, who probably wondered why I took so long to offer "dash," I buckled my seat belt for the flight to Lorenzo Marques.

Mozambique was at that time a Portuguese colony and its capital was big city squalor at its worse. There being no hotels in the airport area, I received assistance to call a taxi to take me to a downtown hotel.

After more than an hour wait at the airport, I assumed a communication mix-up occurred and boarded a city bus with the hope that it would get me to the city center.

After about 15 minutes on the bus, there was some commotion caused by a taxi blocking the bus's path after which the taxi driver came aboard and angrily made his way towards my seat. While I do not speak Portuguese, the other passengers as well as myself had not the least doubt about what triggered his anger. With embarrassment and apologies to all, none of whom could understand what I was saying, I disembarked and rode the man's taxi to a modest hotel in the city center. I gave him a generous tip.

The following morning, the hotel arranged for a taxi to take me to the airport for a pleasant charter flight with a sober pilot to beautiful and mountainous Mbabane, Swaziland, where a dozen bright young students were selected for a US university experience.

The only danger here was the deadly mamba snake found everywhere. I was advised that when walking on any path, I should remain as far from the edge as possible.

The trip out of Africa was uneventful save for the four-hour delay in the Portuguese-held Luanda, Angola airport. As the only American on the plane, I was the only one not allowed to leave the dirty, hot, and disorganized terminal area to visit Luanda. Instead, I walked the streets of the village near the terminal. Anti-Americanism was alive and thriving in Angola!

It was a memorable experience and the Boston ASPAU office was delighted that I had completed the selection process successfully.

On a trip loaded with interesting memories, there was one more before my arrival at the Detroit airport. It was a TWA flight from Lisbon, Portugal. With the DC-10 half full and the doors open awaiting the arriving passengers, the overhead oxygen masks suddenly dropped down. There was a bit of a panic but another

American seated across the aisle from me and I agreed that there was no need to don the masks. The cabin door was open!

A young American couple occupying the seats in front of me felt differently. Influenced by fear they neglected to unhook their seatbelts as they tried desperately to reach for their oxygen masks. The young man with his stretch was able to connect with the mask while she cried! He ignored her while "saving" himself.

If they were on their honeymoon, the incident would surely lead to a brief marriage. They were both very quiet on our flight to the Motor City.

CLANDESTINE ADVENTURE IN LAGOS (1968)

In 1968 Nigeria was a nation rich in oil but weak on sharing its wealth with its citizenry. The country was politically divided between the Muslim-dominated Fulanis of the north who had a major influence on the government and the industrious and business-minded Ibos of the south and eastern part of the country. Their conflict during the 1960's led to the internal Biafra War as the Ibos demanded independence.

Lagos was a nervous community with military personnel challenging outsiders on the streets that were frequently blacked out at nighttime because of air raids. The Ibo "air force" which consisted of a twin-engine prop plane frequently dropped petroleum bombs (Molotov cocktails) on Lagos.

I visited Lagos to interview candidates for admission to prestigious US universities under the African Scholarship Program of American Universities (ASPAU.) My host was the head of the US-sponsored African American Institute in Lagos.

When our assignment was completed late one morning, my in-country host, Ron, his wife, their two very young children, and I crossed the Lagos Lagoon to visit Tarkwa Bay for a swim in the Atlantic Ocean.

While it was an enjoyable outing, the return to my hotel, the Bristol in mid-Lagos, was a bit late and rather exciting. Because of the serious political unrest in Nigeria at that time, no ferries operated after about 5:00 PM. The Lagoon was two or three hundred meters wide and our return route had to be over the waterway.

As darkness fell, we began the long trek in search of a tribesman with a canoe who might be willing to take us to the other shore. With one child on Ron's shoulders, the other with his hand clasped to his mother's, and me following, we trudged through the unfamiliar and unfriendly terrain of muck, tall grass, some trash, and other obstacles for an hour during which we pleaded unsuccessfully with a number of Nigerians to provide us with transportation.

Finally, enough "dash" (bribe) was offered to a tribal member who made the five in of us lie prone in his large canoe while he paddled us to a hotel pier. From there, we made our way walking through unlit streets to Ron's vehicle some two miles distant. Occasionally we would collide with or stumble over a person seated on the walkways. With my hand firmly on my wallet pocket I arrived at the Bristol Hotel slightly tanned from the beach and much relieved to be back safely.

CLIMBING HUAYNA PICCHU (1971)

A group of about 30 university and US State Department personnel along with a few spouses, convened in Lima, Peru for a continent-wide workshop on foreign student admissions to US colleges and universities. At the completion of the workshop, most participants opted for a flight to Cuzco, the ancient Inca capital, followed by a train / bus trip to the famed Inca settlement of Machu Picchu.

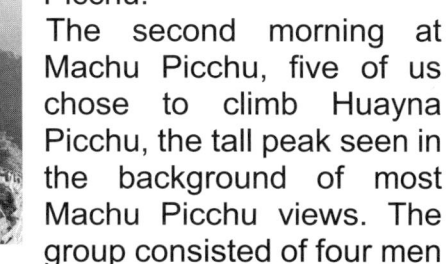

The second morning at Machu Picchu, five of us chose to climb Huayna Picchu, the tall peak seen in the background of most Machu Picchu views. The group consisted of four men and one female spouse, Maria. We soon realized that safety standards that protect tourists in the US had not yet reached the Andean range. It was a perilous trek! A careless step on a slippery or loose rock and you might end up several hundred feet below in the Urubamba River or on an inaccessible ledge. Such accidents were common; especially in the 1970s before additional safety elements were in place. Today, one must register, pay a fee, and wait in line to undertake the much safer trip up Huayna Picchu.

Our group occupied all of the rooms of the area's hotel facilities so we had Machu Picchu and the peak all to ourselves until the noon bus arrived from the base of the mountain.

The 90-minute climb consisted of pathways, a few stone steps, areas of cables strung between stakes for handgrips, and a tunnel approaching the summit that required a crawl on hands and knees. The summit was a rounded stone with an unfenced "safe area" of about 30 feet by 30 feet. Beyond that area, the slope and smoothness of the rock would make a return to the safe area difficult.

The view from the top was breathtaking! The Machu Picchu ruins looked like a child's play set. The long, winding road to the Inca settlement gave one an appreciation of the engineering challenge to make the area accessible for all. That feat was, however, miniscule compared to the incredible challenge faced by the early Incas who created Machu Picchu. It is a classic example of how early indigenous societies were able to build intelligently designed water supplies, agricultural, living, and social systems in geographically demanding terrains.

Our return down the peak was not without some excitement. Maria suffered a panic attack on the summit and was led down under the firm clasp of a climbing partner. Three of us alternated ten-minute shifts helping Maria during the two-hour descent.

Maybe it was the altitude, a competitive spirit, or maybe it was a mental process that pushes one towards achieving a goal even though common sense might suggest after a few yards into the trek, that it was not going to be simply another walk in the park. Each of us had the feeling early on that maybe we should allow good judgment to prevail and return to the base. That feeling was intensified on the return down the slope. It was more nerve shattering, as the descent required looking down rather than up.

The sense of adventure is a powerful motivator, however, and even Maria was glad that she took on and almost conquered the mighty Huayna Picchu.

NAVIGATING CHECK-POINT CHARLIE (1972)

While in Berlin, Germany, on assignment, I took advantage of the location to visit Stockholm to work with Swedish colleagues on plans for a Nordic Country credential evaluation workshop that I was to direct later that year. In a stroke of bad luck, my Berlin departure date was on maybe the only time ever that all European and US airlines went on strike.

After conferring with US Embassy staff, it was suggested that if I was adventurous, I might want to try the Schonefeld airport in East Berlin. It was the time of the infamous Iron Curtain and the Berlin Wall when the Russian and German Democratic Republic (GDR) governments did not welcome western visitors.

With a "special consideration" letter from the embassy and a car and a driver, I headed for Berlin's Check-Point Charlie, the heavily guarded access between the two unfriendly populations. After a lengthy questioning by GDR guards, I was transported by a GDR military vehicle to the airport. I soon realized (and should have known!) that there were no special services for English speakers and virtually all signs were in German. I finally found a ticketing desk and was led to a currency exchange booth where my dollars were converted into GDR marks. After I secured a ticket I found my departure gate and was pleased to be assigned a seat next to an English-speaking Swede.

On the flight from East Berlin to Stockholm, I had an interesting conversation with the Swedish businessman who, upon learning that my grandparents emigrated from Sweden during the 1890s, proclaimed that they "must have been very courageous and very intelligent." Surprised by his generalization, but fully willing to accept it, I asked him to explain. He responded with "They were smart enough to leave Sweden at that time and brave enough to go where few spoke their language."

He continued by explaining that the migration to America was a time when many Swedes, mostly promising young men, sought to unshackle themselves from the restrictive Swedish society and pursue their ambitions elsewhere. (So much for the Statue of Liberty with its oft quoted phrase, "send me your poor, your weak, your down trodden …")

The adventure continued at our arrival at Stockholm's Arlanda Airport. Because of the airline strike, nobody was available to handle the luggage. The airport was uncomfortably quiet because of the lack of travelers. My new friend and I were among a few passengers who climbed ladders to retrieve the luggage from the aircraft and transport it to the arrival authorities for clearance.

NINE COUNTRIES IN ELEVEN DAYS (1975)

One of my more memorable Overseas School Project assignments was my eleven-day trip in East Asia with good friend, Sterling "Sandy" Huntley, Admissions Director at Cal Tech. Our US Department of State sponsors assumed that we would divide the travel, which would leave us to carry out the school visit process alone. We figured, however, that with careful scheduling, we could cover the nine countries in eleven days together thereby giving each school the advantage of a two-man team visit.

While such an ambitious schedule would be nearly impossible today, it was doable during that fall of 1975. Planes were seldom full and hopping from one flight to another was easily done without penalty. It was completed with carry-on luggage, which required frequent launderings. Because we usually stayed in host country homes occupied by teachers, their maids would wash and dry the clothes while we worked, although my washed socks in Kuala Lumpur had to be hung up in Jakarta and Singapore before they were completely dry.

A typical visit would consist of a 5:00 AM wake-up and breakfast, an embassy car transport to the airport for our 8:00 AM departure for a two-hour flight. An embassy or school car would meet us at our destination and take us to the school for an all-day program of lectures, conferences with counselors and administrators, and a few individual interviews.

At 4:00 PM, we would be taken to our host home or hotel to unpack, rest, and dress for a 6:00 PM dinner. That was followed by a college night program for students and parents and, after politely refusing after dinner drinks and conversation with staff, we were returned to our sleeping facility at 10:00 PM. This plan would take us to Tokyo, then on to Taipei, Hong Kong, Manila, Kuala Lumpur, Jakarta, Singapore, Bangkok, and Seoul.

While we experienced many event filled days, a most memorable one for me was our last night in Seoul. I watched the UM / Ohio State game on the Armed Forces Network in my hotel room. Kick-off was at 2:30 AM. We lost 21-14 after taking a 14 to 0 lead at the half.

At 6:30 AM with no sleep and the defeat on my mind I made my way to the coffee shop, where I happened to come face to face in a hall with a group of Japanese business men who smiled and returned my sleepy-eyed "good morning" with their polite and proper Japanese response, "Oha-yoo," which sounded to me much like that "team down south." I hope that they failed to notice my frown!

UNINTENDED HEROICS (1976)

While on an assignment in Tokyo, Japan I accepted an invitation to lecture on US college admission issues with students enrolled at St. Mary's International School. With hundreds of mostly American students, their parents, and school staff in attendance, I noted some restlessness amongst the audience. Assuming that an underground train had caused the building vibration and noise, I continued on without pause.

At the conclusion of my comments, two nuns approached me at the podium with arms extended for a warm handshake and an expression of appreciation for my performance. I soon learned, however, that their praise was not for my comments, but for my calm demeanor during a minor earthquake!

My response was simply, "Earthquake?"

It seems that even tremors in that earthquake-prone country will often generate group panic that can lead to injuries.

With a twinkle in her eye, one nun said quietly "Let's just let everyone continue to think that you are a hero." I would never argue with a nun!

SKI IRAN (1977)

My mission to Iran consisted of working with Iranian educators to examine ways of improving the admission and placement procedures of students seeking enrollment in US universities and colleges. The US Department of State personnel were concerned over the large concentration of Iranian students enrolled in junior/community colleges in US rural areas. Many of those institutions were of marginal quality that offered few if any foreign student services, but needed tuition money to exist.

Iran, formerly Persia, was among my most memorable international assignments. Intelligent, sophisticated folks who are very proud of their colorful history populate the country. My first two-week visit in January 1977 was a solo trip to gather facts and assess the local conditions. I conferred mostly with local educators at both secondary and post-secondary levels, Iranian government officials, and US Embassy staffs.

My Teheran hotel was on a busy corner where I could look over the embassy walls from my room. On a day off, I decided to take the long walk to Teheran's Kasbah (old market place.) Anything can be bought, sold, traded, and borrowed there. Thousands of people crowded around hundreds of selling stalls bartering and smoking tobacco with strange odors. After several hours observing Iranian business activity, I decided to return to my hotel.

Taxis are uncommon in Teheran. Transporting around downtown requires standing in the street hailing small personal autos with a destination sign in their window. Aggressiveness pays off, so a tourist unfamiliar with the process will often end up walking long distances.

After a 20-minute trial, a friendly young Iranian jumped to my rescue by stepping in front of a little car and pleading with the driver to take me on. During the trip, the three other riders conversing in Farsi shared their friendly smiles with me. Oh, how I wished I knew what they were talking about. When I departed their company I heard a few English words; welcome, good-bye, enjoy our city, etc.

A highlight was a ski trip to the Dizin Ski Resort in the Alborz Mountains about a two-hour drive north of Teheran. A US Embassy Officer was delighted to learn of my skiing interest and offered the loan of an embassy car, driver, and his wife for a day on the slopes of Dizin. It seems that no one on the embassy staff was a skier, so his Illinois wife was delighted to have the opportunity of an American to accompany her. I was told that Iranian women would not visit ski slopes alone.

It was a terrible ski area characterized by ungroomed hills, no trees, protruding rocks, and runs designed on ridges in a way that forced the skier to nearly always traverse the good fall line lest he ski off into some "unchartered" territory!

My follow-up visit to Iran in June was again with my good friend Stirling Huntley, of Cal Tech. We visited Isfahan and Shiraz and met with many fine people. I would like one day to return to mysterious and exciting Iran.

(In November, 1979, two years after my second visit to Iran, local activists invaded the US Embassy and captured and held 52 Americans for 444 days. That event resulted in a severance of official relationships between the two countries that continues to exist.)

SKIING AT LA PARVA IN THE ANDES (1978)

Santiago, Chile is a European-style city in almost every sense except location. On an educational assignment during their winter season I took advantage of a weekend to ski at La Parva, located about 60 minutes from the city.

Shortly before my arrival in Chile, the local currency (*escudo*) suffered a serious devaluation. With my wad of dollars, I was able to dine in the best restaurants and be lodged in the city's best hotel at a tenth of the cost of a comparable experience in the US. I succumbed to the temptation and signed up for an all-expense paid weekend ($15) at the La Parva Ski Resort. That tidy sum included transportation, one nights lodging, food and wine, ski rentals, and lift tickets. I could have purchased a pair of Head Master skis for about $12. I chose to not take more advantage of their currency crisis.

There were two major disappointments at La Parva. First, the slopes were in terrible shape. I met an American and we decided to sidestep part way up the mountain slope to make it somewhat more manageable for skiing. Even so, I fell twice and my new friend fell several times. On one of his "eggbeaters," his wig left his head, shocking me, as it first appeared that maybe a sharp piece of ice shaved off the top of his head.

The second surprise came as I checked into my room before the evening meal. It was a large room with 10 or 12 double bunk beds. Because the area is so close to Santiago, few skiers remain overnight so it was the only lodging available at La Parva. Most of the inn guests were women and most had brought their sleeping bags with them. For my US currency, I was able to rent nice bedding for one dollar, but the sleeping sounds of 20 roommates made it a long night for me.

How would I explain to my wife that one night I shared a room with a dozen women?

SHAVING CREAM APPLIED IN AMMAN (1984)

They say that timing is everything and I did not pick a good time to fly from Amman, Jordan to Kuwait City. Before I departed my hotel that morning, I learned that Yasser Arafat, the founding father of Palestinian nationalism and generally recognized as a world terrorist, had been denied a visitor's visa by the US government. He had been invited to address the United

Nations assembly in New York. The hotel staff in Amman warned me that I could expect some harassment at the airport. They were right.

All went swimmingly until I approached security. Flying on an Arab airline from one Arab city to another, I found myself the only recognizable westerner in the security area. Smiles graced the faces of both security staff and fellow travelers as they contemplated some kind of a revenge activity. All of my belongings were in a carry-on valet bag and a brief case.

After a lengthy series of superfluous questions, my valet bag was opened and everything removed. As other travelers and staff crowded around to witness the drama, a security officer opened my shaving kit and proceeded to spray my foamy shaving cream on a suit, neckties, and some shirts. He then awaited a response from me, hoping, I suspect, for a display of anger from me, which would give him cause to run me in. I merely smiled with the others, politely thanked them in Arabic (*shukran*) and was passed on without further incident, hoping that my clothing was not ruined.

Happily, both my belongings and I arrived at my destination in good shape.

CARPET PURCHASES IN LAHORE (1985)

Arriving early one morning in Lahore, a large city in central Pakistan near the Indian border, I was met at the airport by a US Consulate driver and whisked to the Lahore American School. After a full day of speeches to groups of students and consultations with staff and American families, I was invited to the home of the US Consul General of Lahore for a cocktail party. Attending the party at the historic mansion were several consulate officials, school administrators, and a few prominent Americans and Europeans residing in the community.

While I have attended countless such functions on my travels throughout the world for the College Board / US State Department project, this was one of the most memorable.

The wandering tribes of the southern sections of Pakistan, Afghanistan and Iran weave some of the world's most valued handmade carpets. Our host provided his guests with the opportunity to view and purchase some of those rugs in his home. Four Pakistanis in two pick-up trucks delivered to his living room several hundred rugs, ranging in size from approximately 2' by 3' to 6' by 8.' Several stacks of rugs of similar sizes were placed on the floor.

While munching snacks and sipping wine, the guests stood by watching the workers go through a stack of rugs, one by one. They set aside any that were signaled by a guest as one of interest. Those not set aside were returned to the truck and the much smaller piles would then be viewed again with the same signal system. After two or three more repeats only a few remained. All piles of rugs would be examined similarly.

The bargaining began first with the vendor setting the minimum amount. Most carpets went to a solo bidder. Occasionally, competitive bidding between two or more guests would take place, which led to the party entertainment. The alcohol-enhanced process raised both the laughter and the noise levels and to the delight of the sellers many rugs were purchased.

Because I missed opportunities to purchase tribal rugs during previous trips to Iran, I was determined to not go home empty handed this time. I bought a nice 5' by 7' Baluchistan and a 4' by 6' carpet woven by another tribe.

Soon after the purchase, I was faced by another challenge. Much to my disappointment, some Americans at the reception advised me that the local postal system could not be trusted and that I would need to tote my purchases back to Ann Arbor via checked baggage.

I was able to get my carpets tightly rolled together, rope tied and with a rope grip to carry the 40-pound parcel. Unfortunately, my assignment included additional two-day visits to Delhi and Bangkok, followed by overnights in Hong Kong and San Francisco before my final touch down in Detroit. Only in Delhi was I instructed to untie the rugs for inspection by customs officials.

We enjoy the rugs, but I remain unsure whether or not the physical and logistical effort to bring them home was worth it!

NEW YORK, NEWYORK! MY KIND OF TOWN

While serving in the USN in 1949, I chanced with friends to view the movie, "On the Town," a classic musical. It was about three sailors ashore in the "Big Apple" starring Frank Sinatra and Gene Kelly, who, with another sailor and three beautiful female co-stars, danced and sang their way around that great city.

With my buddies, Steve and Joe, we ventured ashore with the hopes of having a similar experience. Of course we failed, probably because we lacked singing and dancing skills as well as the good looks and charms of Frank and Gene.

After a few unsuccessful visits to adult drink establishments, we dropped in to a below the street surface place where we were treated to a beer as we sat down. Our moment of joy quickly changed, however, as we noted that all of the patrons of the dimly lit bar were men, mostly smiling. We immediately left a small tip and departed. Frank and Gene were unchallenged!

Since that initial visit, I have made several dozen trips to New York and have fond memories of that prodigious city.

A single bus ride from West 58th or 59th Street across town and then southbound on 2nd Avenue to 14th street took about 40 minutes on a "local" bus. At my first stop only standing room was available for passengers. The bus was disconcertingly quiet.

When an arriving middle aged woman clutched an overhead strap for safety I arose and offered her my seat. I noted a few curious looks. After a minute or two, the then seated lady looked up at me and with a distinct New York nasal voice, and said,

"You ain't from New Yawk, are you?"

"No, Ma'am, I'm from Michigan."

A fellow standing near me voiced,

"I have an uncle in Toledo. That's near Michigan, isn't it?"

"Yep, it's pretty close."

A very elderly lady with a big hat who I thought should be sitting added,

"I was in Michigan once. I think it was Detroit."

"What you doin' in New York?" asked a seated healthy looking gent who I thought should have offered his seat to the elderly big hatted lady.

"Meetings."

Therein, began a conversation of several passengers that lasted most of the trip.

New Yorkers were talking with New Yorkers, at first mostly about their Michigan connections. Passengers arrived while others departed, but the conversation continued. By the time we reached 14th Street, Michigan was not mentioned but folks were still talking. I enjoyed listening with an occasional comment.

During this entire episode, conversations were almost totally "one liners" and spoken mostly without a smile or any indication that a friendship was underway.

That experience suggested to me that in our nation's most populated city, people are lonely and willingly engage in conversations if started by someone else, usually a visitor.

After that experience, my numerous trips to the Big Apple would always include a cup of coffee in a modest restaurant where I would compliment the waitress on her good service and the quality of her coffee. Then, I would find, that my cup would always be filled and I would be addressed as "hon!"

Another story embedded in my mind I like to call "Sjogren's New York." Because my many New York visits were mostly for meetings, I was often asked by my colleagues to suggest evening entertainments. I had a mental list of good NYC jazz clubs, interesting restaurants, museums, people-watching sites, and "watering holes" better known as bars.

After I led a group of five or six colleagues to two places without anything of interest I feared that my good reputation was going to take a serious hit.

"But don't despair, friends. This is Sjogren's New York," I voiced!

It happened in a small below street-level place on East 41st.Street. After a few sips of our adult beverages, the door opened and several cast members of a Broadway musical entered following their show. They gathered around the piano and began singing old show tunes. We were invited to join the party for a night of good music, funny stories, and new acquaintances. With my good reputation now restored, we left the place at mid-night with smiles of satisfaction.

I like New Yorkers and their great city!

VISITING EAST ASIA IN A PRIVATE JET (1993)

One of my most memorable assignments occurred in 1993, my final year as dean of admissions and financial aid at the University of Southern California. I was invited to join a team of six senior USC administrators for a two – week sojourn to Asia. An alumnus provided his *Gulfstream 4* jet and all expenses for visits to Tokyo, Taipei, Jakarta, Singapore, Hong Kong, and Seoul. I and one other official were alone on the Jakarta and Singapore legs.

Our primary mission was to meet with and seek financial support from USC's alumni clubs. I was along to visit American and home country secondary schools to recruit students, along with attending the major functions. Because of previous visits to most of the schools I had visited under the US State Department sponsorship, I was well acquainted with the schools and their staffs.

At the various landing sites an airport limousine would great us at the plane and transport us to a V.I.P. entrance where our arrival formalities and baggage check were handled quickly.

There was no spending limit! We stayed in upgraded rooms in the best hotels. I would be transported to the schools by a hotel car with a driver. Food and drink of the highest quality would be served both during the events and when we were "on our own."

What a way to end a career! It's highly unlikely that any other college admissions guy has had a similar experience.

Gulfstream 4 Aircraft (seats 15)

AN AIRMAN TURNS SUBMARINER (1993)

After a brief journey on a submarine in Key West in 1949, I felt fortunate to have been assigned to an aircraft carrier. Sailors walking in the submarine's narrow foot traffic areas would find it difficult to pass a shipmate without touching him. (It's no wonder that submarines were about the last duty assignment for female sailors.)

In 1993 when the US Navy in Long Beach, CA invited six senior administrators, three each from USC and UCLA, for a few hours sail in an atomic submarine, the USS Guardfish. I was selected.

The highlight of the trip was in the navigation station with its control wheel and periscope. When the tour director officer asked if there was a navy veteran among the guests, I was the only one to step forward. After I described my USN responsibilities, a rather loud and nervous "Oh, no! Not another airdale!" was heard throughout the cabin. (US Navy sailors assigned to an air base or aircraft carrier were called "air dales" by the USN's non-airmen.)

With my already fear-driven wet hands I clasped the lateral handle that controlled the periscope. When ordered to turn slowly to starboard, several crewmen fell down or bumped against the bulkhead. One sailor yelled, "Look out! You're going to run into Hawaii!" Another voiced words not fit for family readers.

Of course, it was an act, but it struck instant fear into my heart. My civilian colleagues were much amused over the incident.

USS Guardfish (SSN-612)

As I departed the vessel I was given a card that reads:

"Be it known to all good sailors of the Seven Seas that Cliff Sjogren on March 26, 1990 was this date totally submerged in the United States Submarine USS Guardfish SSN 612.
In consequence of such dunking and his initiation into the mysteries of the deep he is hereby designated as an
"Honorary Submariner".

PART THREE: RETIREMENT

TRAVERSE CITY (1993 - 2001)

While our four-year California experience was a highly positive one, we were happy to return to our lakeside home in Traverse City. The next eight years included frequent visits with family and friends and several vacation trips throughout the US and abroad. I continued my volunteer commitments with the National Collegiate Athletic Association, the International Baccalaureate, and the College Board. Pat accompanied me on several assignments.

Most importantly, it was a period of our family's major expansion! Our first grandson, Justin, was born on August 31, 1984 in Alpena. It would be 12 years before Wesley the second one arrived on April 14, 1996 in Petoskey. The next day, April 15, in the same Petoskey hospital and served by the same physician, Andrew and Jacob were born. Just short of three months later, Peter and Brita were born in Denver on July 13, 1996.

Claire was born August 10, 1998 in Traverse City and William entered the world September 5, 2002 in Royal Oak when the family resided in Novi.

Much of our time in Traverse City was spent cruising our pontoon boat on beautiful Long Lake. Many close friends lived on the lake's shores including several of my CMU fraternity brothers. Every two years we would have a reunion at a "brother's" lakeside home and serenade our significant others with such tunes as:

*You put her in a corner and hold her tight like this.
You put your arms around her waist
and on her lips a kiss.
And if she starts to murmur or if she
starts to sigh,
Just tell her it's the well-known seal of Delta Sigma Phi!*

We enjoyed our years in Traverse City but we were ready to go home. We wanted a small town environment and a closer relationship with our family and longtime friends.

CADILLAC (2001 -)

We returned to Cadillac in March 2001 and purchased a two-acre lot in Wedgewood, located off 33 Mile Road a mile south of M-55. Our temporary rental housing was the owner's house at Watt's Motel on Mackinaw Trail.

We engaged a Traverse City architect and a McBain builder to erect our Wedgewood home. After several frustrating months of trying to work out building costs and details, we decided to cancel construction and find a place to buy closer to town.

We found it across the street from our rental site. We moved into our retirement home at 7774 Mackinaw Trail in September 2001, the week of the World Trade Center destruction by terrorists. The home had nearly 4,000 feet of finished living area, including a large walkout lower level, which was enjoyed by the grandchildren during their frequent visits. Located on McGuire's Golf course, the site provided a beautiful view of the lake and the forests beyond.

Between numerous family visits to St. Ignace and Novi with a few to Littleton and Breckenridge, Colorado, we enjoyed many family and travel experiences both in the US and abroad.

We bought a winter home in the huge retirement community at 3583 Worth Circle, The Villages, in Central Florida. We soon decided that we liked Michigan better and sold that place six months after the purchase.

We have attended several Elderhostels, mostly in the Southeast US and had three month-long visits in Green Valley, Arizona.

On October 10, 2014 our lives changed radically. It was necessary to have Pat admitted to the Curry House Assisted Living and Memory Care facility in Cadillac. She began to show signs of cognitive impairment about two years preceding the Curry House admission. We began early to prepare for the change by selling our Mackinaw Trail home and purchasing a condo on my beloved Lake Cadillac shore. We moved in during early July 2014, about three months before our altered lives.

We have enjoyed a very good life together. That pretty girl with green eyes captured my heart in Mr. Nelson's history class in 1942. Now after 11 years as a friend followed by 63 years of marriage, I find that my love for her grows stronger each day.

OUR EIGHT GRANDCHILDREN
Photo taken at Crystal Mountain Resort, June 2014

(L to R) **Justin**, *a Clinical Biostatistician/ Programmer, holds a Bachelors and a Master degree, both with Honors from Grand Valley State U.* **Wesley** *will enroll at MSU or CMU in 2017 as a transfer.* **Andrew** *(MSU,)* **Jacob**, *(U of M,)* **Peter**, *(U of Edinburgh, Scotland,) and* **Brita**, *U. of Colorado) are all juniors at university.* **Claire** *is a MSU freshman and* **William** *will be a ninth grader at Milford HS in September 2017.*

DETROIT TURKEY TROTS
(2013, 2015 and 2016)

My more recent 'athletic" achievement took place on the streets of downtown Detroit. My family convinced me to participate in the 2015 Annual Thanksgiving Day Turkey Trot. It is a fun-filled event where most entrants view the "trot" as a social gathering. The 19,000 participants of the 5K and 10K contests walk, trot, or run through the Motor City streets past thousands of spectators who have lined the sidewalks for the Thanksgiving Day Parade. There were nine Sjogrens in the event. With my numbered bib and its attached ID computer chip, my walking "sticks," and dressed in a sweatshirt and shorts, I awaited the launch time for my wave of contestants. My son, Sigurd, accompanied me. (Don't be confused. I also had a great uncle, an uncle, and a brother by that Swedish given name.)

The results: I placed first of the entire 19,000 in the number of years lived (87) and second best time in my age category. (Important detail: Only three of the 5K runners were in the "Over 80 Years" category and the others were youngsters at 81.)

In my first "Turkey Trot" in 2013, I tied for first in age at 85 among only three contestants over 80 years of age.

After the 2015 race, I was advised that the Cadillac High School Marching Vikings defeated 11 competing bands for first place honors in Detroit's Thanksgiving Day Parade. That "victory" filled me with much more pride than did my pleasant ramble down the streets of Detroit.

At my third Turkey Trot (2016), I was again the oldest competitor at age 88. The next oldest was a youngster of 82.

(I am left wondering why they would name a one-way street "Clifford.")

NATIONAL VOLUNTEER ACTIVITIES

Three of my professional association activities continued for about 10 years after my retirement from USC. I remained as chair of the National Collegiate Athletic Association committee on the Foreign Student Credential Evaluation, a position I held since its inception 20 years earlier. It consisted of at least two meetings each year at sites selected by our five-person group.

I was also retained as a Board member of the International Baccalaureate of North America, a position I had held for about 25 years. That role had me visit secondary schools throughout the US, Canada, and the Caribbean Sea area where I led teams to approve schools for IB participation, monitored IB examinations, and participated in Board meetings.

Finally, I continued involvement with the American Association of Collegiate Registrars and Admission Officers, including the management for several weeks of the central office in Washington. At recent annual meetings of AACRAO, I have been the last past president introduced at the opening sessions. My term of presidency was in 1981-82, about 34 years before this writing. Of course the audience is told to hold their applause until all past presidents have been introduced. (I enjoy being the only one to receive the applause!)

When volunteering as a retiree, Pat traveled with me on many NCAA, IBNA, and AACRAO assignments where we would often extend the trip for several days as tourists. We especially enjoyed our trips to Canada from Vancouver to Nova Scotia. A lengthy visit in the Bahamas was also memorable.

LOCAL VOLUNTEER ACTIVITIES

After leaving Traverse City for Cadillac in 2001, I decided to redirect my volunteer activities towards my hometown needs. I delivered meals to live-ins for the Shepherds Table of the First Baptist Church, assisted the library several times with used book sales, the book giveaways for Project Christmas, and collected contributions at storefronts for the Salvation Army's Christmas red bucket project.

My primary volunteer contribution, however, was and continues to be, volunteer work for the Wexford County Historical Society and Museum. (WCHS.)

It began on a summer day in about year 2004. On a visit to the WCHS museum, I noted that sunrays were shining directly on several 100-year old local historical photographs scattered about on a table. As a former US Navy aerial photographer, I mentioned my concern to a woman standing nearby. The conversation went something like this:

"The museum staff is being careless with these important images of our history."
"What would you suggest to the staff?'"
"Scan the photos and wrap the originals in acid-free tissue, place them in acid-free boxes, and store them in a darkened climate-controlled facility. Sort and write descriptions about the images, create a museum Website, and enter the photos and descriptions on the site for all to view."
"Would you be willing to assist us?"
"Yes."

That woman was Mary Beth Montague, then president of the WCHS. I was asked to attend the next Board meeting held in the Historic District home of Board member, Nan Taylor, where I met nice people and enjoyed very good snacks. Lucky guy! At that meeting I accepted an invitation to become a Board member.

It has been a labor of love! For more than a decade and continuing, there have been countless hours of very enjoyable and satisfying work. My admiration for my community and its history combined with my family's history in Cadillac added further reasons to commit myself to the challenge.

A list of my major WCHS activities follows:

1) Sketched the design for the WCHS Website and with the Cadillac News Staff Website professionals brought it to fruition.
2) Scanned, researched, and wrote titles and descriptions for more than 1,500 early Cadillac area historical scenes and managed their

insertions onto the Website. (I had volunteer assistance collecting and sorting the images.)
3) Contributed two personal celebratory issues of the Cadillac Evening News consisting of more than 200 pages of area history and had them cleaned, de-acidified, placed in acid-free plastic sleeves, and mounted in scrapbooks by the Bentley Historical Library of the University of Michigan. They are in the museum's research room for perusal by visitors. Jack Westman, a friend, and a Cadillac High School alumnus, funded that project and several others.
4) Researched and wrote the Website entry, Wexford County History, with links to some important digitized historical books on Wexford County.
5) Indexed about 2,500 significant chronology items, 750 full stories, and 167 commercial ads from the 1951 and 1971 celebratory Cadillac Evening News issues and linked them to the Website History page. (Note: The site also includes a lengthy article by Judge William Peterson, author of "The View from Courthouse Hill," that was edited and expanded for the article.)
6) With the Westman grant and several hundred dollars of my personal funds, I purchased a screen and projector for free narrated slide presentations throughout the Cadillac area. I have presented over 70 narrated slide shows in Wexford and Osceola counties.
7) With the Westman grant, I had the two celebratory issues of the newspaper digitized and microfilmed by the Clarke Historical Library on Central Michigan University's campus. I donated one of the two-microfilmed copies to the Cadillac News. Those two issues can now be read online via the WCHS site.

8) Because the site is word and name searchable, it has been receiving an average of more than 300 "hits" a day. At this writing, the total has exceeded 435,000 total "hits". I responded to hundreds of inquiries posted by Website viewers.

9) Wrote a book on the Cadillac area early history, "Timber Town Tales," that soon became the bestselling book ever at the Cadillac Horizon Book Store. I funded the printing of the book and all profits from sales are contributed to the Wexford County Historical Society and Museum. It has appeared three times as Number One and twice at Number Two on the Traverse City Record Eagle weekly North West Michigan Best Sellers list in the paperback non-fiction category. During the first year, more than 1,000 copies were sold. The book has so far generated thousands of dollars for the museum from sales, donations for printing and mailing, and both "in kind" and funding donations from members of the community and the Cadillac Printing Company.

All profits from book sales, my narrated presentations, special writing projects for which honoraria are awarded, etc. have been and will continue to be bestowed to the Wexford County Historical Society and Museum.

CONCLUDING STATEMENT

Shakespeare once penned, "What's past is prologue." That profound observation suggests that with an understanding of our history, both family and beyond, we may discover more about who we are and what makes us act the way we do. The process of writing this life story and an earlier book about the history of my community, has given me some insights into why I possess certain behavior patterns, social attitudes, and life priorities.

Let's all study a little history. It enriches the mind!

APPENDIX ONE: FAMILY HISTORY

SJOGREN AND GOULD FAMILY HISTORIES

Sjögrens in Sweden (19th century)

Note: *Much of the material that follows is either directly quoted, or summarized, from research completed by my Father, Clifford "Cap" Sjogren, Sr. and my Mother, Pauline Gould Sjogren. Their visit to Sweden in the 1960's enabled them to get first-hand accounts of the early days of the family. My Father's ability to speak Swedish, albeit with a definite 19th century syntax, was of great benefit to them as they were able to gather and display in a highly-organized way, the results of their research. Their information was compiled in two scrapbooks, together with priceless photographs. My brother, Sigurd, and I possess those valuable family assets.*

In 1894 Frans Adolph Fridolph Sjögren (1874-1940) of Hemse, Gotland Province, Sweden, emigrated to the US and made his way to the Baldwin, Michigan area to work in the lumber camps. At about the same time, Ida Maria Eriksson (1875-1954,) of Heby, Uppsala Province, Sweden, arrived in Ludington, Michigan, with her aunt and uncle. Frans found employment at a lumber harvesting community, Sisson Lilly, a few miles south of Baldwin.

The translation of the name, Sjögren, combines two common Swedish terms. *Sjö* means "lake" or "sea" or "body of water." *Gren* is "branch." One might logically assume, therefore, that our early family members had some association with the nautical trades. Indeed, they did!

The information we have on that branch of the family reveals that Jonas Sjogren was born in 1830 in Vella, Visby, in the Gotland Islands, a thriving port in the Baltic Sea. Jonas married Amalia Eskelund, of nearby Eskelhem, Kinterham, Gotland, who was nearly 20 years younger than Jonas.

Tales of early Viking forays throughout Medieval Europe and the Near East frequently mention Gotland, a derivative of the term "Goths," as a home base for those marauders. Further, historical research reveals strong evidence of Eastern Mediterranean populations including Muslims once populated Gotland.

While not yet validated by documents, conversations between my father and relatives in Sweden suggest that Amalia's grandfather was a sea captain who married a Spanish "girl of royalty" and brought her back to Sweden. If true, that might explain certain "un-Swedish" features of some of us, such as olive-tinctured skin and brown and hazel eyes.

Jonas and Amelia operated a cleaning and dye shop at the rear of their residential lot in Hemse in the southern part of Gotland. Following are brief descriptions of their eight children:

- Fridolf immigrated to America and lived near Baldwin, Michigan. He married a woman named Madison and had a daughter, Mary. The mother died giving birth to Mary and Fridolf died a few years later. Mary was raised by her grandmother (mother's side) and married Lee Braumbaugh. Mary and Lee had one son and lived in Grand Rapids, Michigan.
- Arvid was a Gotland business man who not only lost his money on poor deals, but his mother's home as well, necessitating her move to Stockholm to live with a daughter. He had olive skin, reflecting his Spanish ancestry, and spelled his name "Sjöögren.

- Frans, (my grandfather) was born in 1874 and immigrated to America where he married Ida Maria Eriksson and fathered eight children.
- Rosa, born in 1877, married a doctor in Gotland and was widowed soon after. She had a son, who died very early, and a daughter, Ann Marie, from her first marriage. She then married Ludwig Seidberg. They had four daughters, Marie, Karon, Mary Ann, and Barbara. Ann Marie gave music lessons for thirty years and Ludwig was an organist in their church for forty years.
- Axel married Hilda. He then left Sweden for America while the children were very young, leaving them with their mother. Their names were Alexis, Gote, Sten, Kjell, Sessan, and Alice.
- Sigurd never married and was living in Cadillac when he died of typhoid fever at age 35. He was living in a boarding on East Mason Street in Cadillac.
- Marta, born in 1886, married a successful banker (Issrelsson) in Stockholm and had two children, Hasse and Maj. Hasse, who died in 1977, and his wife had a daughter, Lena, and a granddaughter Mikael. Maj was engaged to be married, but it never happened. She was a career office secretary.
- Signe, born in 1890, had three children; Stig (wife, Marta,) Karl Gustaf (wife, Stena,) and Karon (husband, Olle Norman). There have been frequent contacts between Karl Gustaf and the American Sjogrens.

Erikssons and Berquists in Sweden (19th Century)

Our information reveals very little about the family of Ida Maria Eriksson, who was to become the wife of Frans Sjogren. *(The umlaut was dropped from "Sjögren" soon after Frans arrived in America.)* Her father, Erik Eriksson, was born August 27, 1850. Erik married Johanna Charlotta Berquist, who was born March 24, 1851. They had two daughters, Ida Maria (my grandmother,) born June 15, 1875 in Molnebo, Heby, and Anna Pauline, born October 28, 1884.

Erik owned and operated an iron foundry in Heby, a small town near the university town of Uppsala, Sweden. When Ida was confirmed, he made the iron gates for the church. Johanna was a licensed mid-wife and was well known throughout Sweden. At that time, Swedish doctors did not deliver babies. In Sweden, every day has a "name." Babies born on that day would assume that name, as well as a second name by a relative. Their parents determined their common given name. That is why Swedes of that time had three given names.

Johanna Berquist had two sisters, Barna and Edla. Barna married John Peterson in Sweden. They had no children. When they immigrated to America in the early 1890s, they took with them their niece, Ida Maria Eriksson (my grandmother.) Edla married Emil Lewis Levine and had two sons in Sweden, Dan and Ellis. They immigrated to America and settled in the Cadillac area. Dan served as chief of police in Cadillac. Erik and Johanna Eriksson eventually brought their daughter, Anna Pauline to Sisson Lily near Baldwin where his older daughter Ida Maria, who had arrived earlier with the Petersons, joined them.

John Peterson's sister, Hedvig, never married, but adopted four children and "gave them good educations." At that time, she was the only woman in Sweden to head a bank and was decorated by the King of Sweden on her 60th birthday. She "received many gifts, letters, and 91 telegrams. The bank gave her a clock and a gold medal for her 30 years of service."

The Children of Frans and Ida Sjogren

Soon after he arrived in America on April 11, 1894, Frans Adolph Sjogren took work as a lumberman in the forests near Sisson Lily, a few miles south of Baldwin, Michigan. He met his wife, Ida Marie Erickson while she was "keeping company" with his brother, Fridolf. Frans was a jolly man with a great sense of humor. He loved his family, especially the children. He and Ida were married in Ludington, Michigan. Their first child, Vivi Lydia Maria, was born in Sisson Lily on March 13, 1895. The small family then moved to Thompsonville, another lumbering community where their son, Sigurd Felix Hildemar, was born on July 27, 1897.

After Thompsonville and a short stay in Cadillac, Frans, Ida, and their two children took up residence in Jennings, a lumber company town about 10 miles northeast of Cadillac. Frans was employed by the Mitchell Brothers Lumber Company. His job consisted of piling lumber in the yards in the winter and painting the company's properties during the summer months.

The workers could buy all of their food and clothing essentials at the company store as long as they did not exceed the wages due to them. They would then receive their check with a corner cut off (known as a "three-cornered check"), which would then be turned in to the cashier at the store and applied to their accounts. During one stretch, Frans worked for eighteen months straight for the "three-cornered" checks. A workweek consisted of six ten-hour days and no vacations. He would often work nights and Sundays for extra spending money.

While in Jennings, Ida gave birth to four more children, my father Frans Gustav Clifford ("Cap"), born June 6, 1901; Eric Arvid Isedorf, born November 30, 1903; Velma Amalia Charlotta, born June 11, 1906; and, Vorni Ranghild Margreta, born July 15, 1909. Frans and Ida and their six children then moved back to Cadillac in 1909 where Rudolf Luther Valentine was born on February 14, 1912 and Frances Ida Vigula was born on April 1, 1917.

Upon his return to Cadillac, Frans went into a private business as a painter and paperhanger. He later opened an automobile paint shop, which would be a losing deal for him. After employment with the Acme Motor Truck Company, he moved to Detroit in 1927 where he joined his son, "Cap" to paint houses and hang wallpaper. When the stock market crashed in 1929, Frans and Ida returned to Cadillac. Frans died on January 8, 1940.

Ida Maria remained in Cadillac at their home at 216 East Nelson Street. She was seldom if ever lonesome as visits by her eight children and many grandchildren were frequent and most welcomed. She remained active in the Zion Lutheran Church located just three doors east of her home. Ida died on March 31, 1954.

Anna Pauline Eriksson, Ida Maria's sister, married Oscar Peterson, of Traverse City. They were married in Jennings, Michigan. Oscar was a cashier at the Mitchell Brothers General Store, the company store in Jennings. Soon after their daughter, Margaret Oscarine, was born they moved to Cadillac where Oscar worked for the County Road Commission and was an agent for the Maccabee Fraternal Lodge. Anna died on January 5, 1956 and Oscar, after having lived for 90 years, died on March 17, 1970.

It is interesting to note that Margaret Oscarine, daughter of Oscar Peterson, married an Oscar Peterson (no relation.)

Except for Rudolf, who spent the final years of his life in Nevada, the eight children of Frans and Ida lived and worked in Michigan their entire lives. It was a highly successful family. The sons all succeeded in their vocational endeavors and the daughters chose husbands who achieved well. Among them were managers of small industrial plants, a senior administrator at a large plant, a small business owner, a construction engineer, a doctor of chiropractic medicine, and salesmen. Three sons served in the military forces, Sigurd in World War I, Clifford soon after World War I, and Rudolph in World War II. The eight children of Frans and Ida fathered (and mothered) seven sons and four daughters.

Vivi Lydia Marie Sjogren Peterson graduated from nursing program at the Augustana Hospital in Chicago. She was a nurse for the victims of the pleasure boat disaster in Lake Michigan near Chicago in which 800 persons drowned! She assisted police with the identification of the dead and collected and tagged jewels. She, with her family, lived on a farm about three miles east of Ludington near the Eagle School. Vivi owned and operated the "Coffee Cup" restaurant and owned "Jack and Jill," a children's shop, in Ludington. Aunt Vivi was a hardworking and very dedicated mother to her three children, Loraine, Bill and Bob.

Sigurd Felix Hildemar Sjogren as a young man worked as a desk clerk at the McKinnon (Northwood) Hotel in Cadillac. He then took employment at the Ireland-Matthew Tool Company in Detroit. He enlisted in the Army Engineers and served in France during World War I. Returning to Michigan after the war, he worked at the desk of the Park Place Hotel in Mt. Clemens, Michigan, where he met his wife-to-be, Jean Clare Kemph of Pittsburgh. They resided in Detroit, where Sigurd worked as a tool and die maker for the Chevrolet

Co. After serving as a salesman at the Columbia Tool Steel Company in Detroit, he was promoted to branch manager, the position he held until he retired. When his wife died, Sigurd returned to Cadillac. Uncle Sig was an unselfish, articulate man, very handsome, and possessor of a great sense of humor.

<u>Clifford ("Cap") Frans Gustav Sjogren</u> (My father, described earlier)

<u>Eric Arvid Isadorf Sjogren</u> went to Detroit at an early age to seek his fortune. He became an assistant credit manager at the Dime Bank in downtown Detroit. He married Kathryn Garret of Virginia. They had no children. He later became manager of the Fenton Tool Co. in Fenton, Michigan where he resided with Kathryn in a very large house. Arvid, it seems, became a bit too "successful" as he experienced some rather serious legal problems late in life. Uncle Arvid always had a big smile and liked to share interesting stories with the family.

<u>Velma Amalia Charlotta Sjogren Marklund</u>, after graduating from Cadillac High School Velma worked as a reporter for the Cadillac Evening News. She later moved to Chicago where she enrolled in the nurses training program at Augustana Hospital. She became a Registered Nurse after three years. Returning to Cadillac, she married Ted Marklund and worked in a doctor's office and the Cadillac Mercy hospital. A back injury suffered while lifting a patient is said to have led to the serious disease, multiple sclerosis. They moved to Detroit (Franklin Hills, two doors from the home of baseball great, Al Kaline), where she was confined to a wheelchair for the rest of her life. Ted remarried and moved to Tennessee. Aunt Velma was an attractive, kind, generous woman who cared very much for her family and friends.

<u>Vornie Ranghild Margreta Sjogren Hoops</u> left Cadillac with her sister, Velma, to begin nurses training at the Augustana Hospital, in Chicago. Her marriage, move to Fenton, Mich., and giving birth to two children, were followed by divorce from her husband, Harold

Hoops. She eventually moved to Flint, Michigan, where she died in a nursing home. Aunt Vornie was very quiet, almost shy, and seemed to be unhappy much of the time.

Rudolph Luther Valentine Sjogren served in the armed forces during World War II. He then went to Detroit where he worked with his brother, Sigurd, selling tool steel. His first wife was Josephine Chapman of Cadillac. They were divorced, without children. He then married Marge Gladstone of Rochester, Michigan with whom he had a daughter, Linda. He moved to Reno, Nevada, where he took his third wife, Dian Cairns, born September 25, 1913. Her mother's name was Victoria Johanson. Dian was a widow with two sons. Rudy died of cancer of the throat. Uncle Rudy, a large handsome man, enjoyed life to its fullest and possessed an engaging sense of humor.

Frances Ida Vigula Sjogren Currier graduated from Cadillac High School and immediately went to Detroit where she enrolled in a course of training to become a beautician. Returning to Cadillac, she worked for Dan Gallivan at his beauty shop. She married George Currier, a chiropractor and son of a major Cadillac furniture storeowner. Aunt Frannie was a very popular and well-liked citizen of Cadillac, attractive and full of fun.

Sjogren Family
Top-Arvid, Velma, Rudy, Vernie, Cap
Bottom-Fran, Sig, Ida, Frank, Vivi

THE EARLY GOULD / WORDEN FAMILY HISTORY

Compared to the Sjogren / Eriksson branch, I have little information about my Mother's family, the Gould / Worden line. Regrettably, dates and important sites are lacking from my family's accumulated notes. There is a need to research the Gould / Warden family linkage to validate the observations that follow and to fill in crucial gaps.

The Goulds

My Grandfather, George Ryerson (Rye) Gould, born August 18, 1862 in Plainfield, Ontario, came to Bay City, Michigan in the 1880s to be with my Grandmother, Margaret Elizabeth Worden (daughter of William H. Warden.) Elizabeth was also born in Plainfield (March 27, 1864.) Soon after their marriage in Bay City on April 19, 1888, Rye and Elizabeth moved to Rosebush, Michigan and purchased a large house. The first four of their five children were born in Rosebush. My Mother, Pauline Mable was born in Cadillac in 1905.

Rye's primary employment was with the Cobbs and Mitchell enterprise in Cadillac. He was an office worker for the company.

Following are quotes with minor editing from my parent's written research document:

"*Rye worked in the lumber mill. Rye's mother came to Rosebush where she lived with another son, Herbert. "Grandma." as the entire community knew her, made friends with everyone. She would go to church every Sunday and always bring guests home for dinner. Rye also had a sister, Jenny, who married Tom Gray. Herbert never married.*

The Wordens

My Grandmother's family the Worden's was a well-to-do clan in Europe. Little is known about Horanson Milburn Worden, the apparent patriarch of the family. He and his wife had three sons, William H., J.E., and Horatio Nelson, and one daughter, Melissa Worden Sonley. J.E. Worden is believed to be the father of Thomas Worden. The following was written to J. E. Warden by his aunt, Mary Jane, in 1912.

"Grandmother Ouelette, from Paris, France, was of a noble family and had to flee to England. The Great Grandfather was Earl of Lorraine. Great Grandmother was Lady Margaret. She married Sir John Francis. The name 'Ouelette' was then called 'Willett.'"

Horatio Nelson Worden married Mary Jane (last name unknown) and they had a daughter, Mary L. There were three or four Worden brothers in Holland all of whom were very rich. One sent his wife to New York with jewels and money. She never arrived as the boat was shipwrecked. Later some of the others departed Holland for Ontario.

J.E. Worden, representing the Worden family, called a meeting in Brighton, Ontario in 1862. All of the relatives met to discuss sending someone to Holland to claim the family's money. They gave up their effort because they couldn't raise the money needed for travel to Europe.

The full story, I should think, would make interesting reading. This is a good example of the frustrations felt by descendants when earlier family members fail to leave written documentation of their life experiences.

My Aunt Pearl Gould nee Hillard remembered the house in Rosebush. It had a large living room. There was no basement under the house. The living room floor was covered with a thick layer of straw under the wall-to-wall carpeting. The straw kept the floor warm in the winter.

Rye worked for the Cobbs and Mitchell Lumber Company in Cadillac for a few years followed by a move to Belding, Michigan where he started a variety store and an ice cream parlor. The Belding business ventures were unsuccessful so he moved back to Cadillac. He purchased the house at 723 Wood Street (now South Mitchell Street) and opened a store near the Lyric Theatre in downtown Cadillac. This store was not successful as well and he returned to work at the mill. Rye died on January 12, 1940 and Elizabeth (Lib) died August 27, 1947. They are buried in Maple Hill Cemetery in Cadillac.

Elizabeth Worden Gould (my grandmother) had two sisters, Melissa (Lis) and Eliza Jane. Melissa remained in Canada and married Thomas Welsh. They made their home in Oshawa, Ontario and had four sons. Harry married Majorie and had two daughters, Elaine and Joanne. Harry was a milk inspector for the Province of Ontario for many years. Oscar and his wife had twins and another boy. Vernon never married. Norman's status is unknown.

Eliza Jane was born on October 18 (year unknown) and married Stephen Woolley of Cadillac. They made their home in Harrietta, Michigan and had four children. William married Nellie and they were both teachers. William was active in youth activities and was a scoutmaster of the Boy Scout troop that Cap (Clifford Sjogren, Sr) belonged to. They had no children. Stephen never married and remained on the farm. Maud married John Eggle. They had a son, Robert. They owned and operated a large farm a few miles south of Cadillac.

Note: *Robert Eggle's grandson, Kris Eggle, Eagle Scout, graduated from Cadillac High School in 1991 as the valedictorian and a track star. Kris enrolled at the University of Michigan and was on the Big Ten Champion cross-country varsity. At the U of M, he studied to be a national park service ranger. Kris was killed while pursuing Mexican drug smugglers at the Organ Pipe Cactus National Monument, Arizona, on August 9, 2002. A Kris Eggle bench in the City Park honors that unusually talented man who made the ultimate sacrifice while in the service of his country.*

Following are brief biographical summaries of the five children of Rye and Elizabeth Gould, taken from Mom and Dad's research.

Ward Percy Gould (b. 2/10/1889; d. 11/19/1966) married Lena Kramer and settled in Belding, Michigan. Ward was a very good musician and played the coronet in the city band. They had six children: Glenn, (no children) lived in Florida, Gertrude, (married Orin Chester Wood and had six children,) Helen (married Aris Haskins, a Pinkerton security guard in Muskegon, had three children,) Mabel, (married Lloyd Gender and had three children,) Dale (background unknown), and George, who was killed as a paratrooper in World War II.

Ward's marriage ended in a divorce and he returned to Cadillac to assume an office position for the Ann Arbor Railroad. He then married Dora LaBar of Cadillac and had a daughter, Pauline, who died soon after birth. Ward was then transferred to Mt. Pleasant and later to Detroit. He eventually moved to Albuquerque, New Mexico where he worked in a large hardware store. After Dora died and was buried in Albuquerque, Ward married Violet McGregory of California. After living together for a month, they divorced and Ward married Exa, her last name unknown. Ward is buried in Albuquerque.

Elgie Edward Gould (b. 7/17/1892; d. 10/25/1955) married Mabel Epson Olson of Cadillac in Belding,

Michigan, 1913. Elgie served in France during World War I. After combat duty, he became the camp barber. After two years of service in the war zone, it was arranged by the Red Cross for him to return home to Belding because of the serious illness of his wife. After she recovered, they moved to Ann Arbor where he became a barber near The University of Michigan campus and the football stadium.

Elgie both managed and played baseball, a sport he continued when he moved to Ann Arbor. Large numbers of spectators attended ball games in those days. Elgie and Mabel had one son, Donald Gould, born January 21, 1924 in Ann Arbor. Donald married Marie Brough in 1943. After World War II naval service, he worked for the Washtenaw County Road Commission as a clerk. Elgie is buried at Arborcrest Cemetery in Ann Arbor.

Elizabeth Pearl Gould (b. 1/26/1894; d. 1/25/1988) married William Hillard in the parlor of her home at 723 Wood Street in Cadillac, October 15, 1913. Pearl was an excellent gardener and her gardens have been featured in local newspapers, with photographs, on at least two occasions. She enjoyed working out of doors and family and friends were always most welcomed in her home.

Will was employed as a deliveryman for the Foster Brothers Company, first with horses and wagons and then Cadillac-made Acme trucks. He was a furniture mover, delivered coal, hunted small game and played a lot of baseball. They had no children. Pearl died in a nursing home west of Kingsley, Michigan and is buried in the Maple Hill cemetery in Cadillac.

George Morely Gould (b 5/29/1902) married Anna Smith on April 19, 1922 in Cadillac. He worked in Cadillac as a grocer and continued the same occupation when he moved to Ann Arbor. He was an excellent left-handed baseball pitcher who seldom lost a game. They had four boys. Richard Morely who died soon after birth, Maurice Kay (an electrician who married Jane Ferguson and had five children,) Dean Carlton, (married Virginia

Du Puis, became an accountant, and moved to Racine, Wisconsin with their four children, and Jerry Lee, an electrician who married Maryann Misuire and fathered four children, all of whom grew up in Ann Arbor.

    Mabel Pauline Gould Sjogren (My mother was described earlier.)

APPENDIX TWO: COUNTRIES VISITED

AMERICAS	EUROPE	ASIA
Argentina (2)	Austria (2)	Bangladesh
Aruba (Neth.) (2)	Azores	Cyprus
Bahamas (3)	Belgium (3)	Guam
Barbados	Crete (Greece)	Hong Kong (**)
Belize (2)	Czech Republic	India (3)
Bolivia	Denmark (4)	Indonesia (3)
Bonaire (Neth.)	England (**)	Iran (2)
Brazil	Finland (2)	Israel (4)
Canada (**)	France (**)	Japan (**)
Chile (2)	Germany, East	Jordan (2)
Columbia (3)	Germany, West (**)	Korea (3)
Costa Rica (3)	Gibraltar (2)	Kuwait (2)
Cuba (3)	Greece (**)	Macao
Curacao (Neth.)	Hungary	Malaysia (3)
Dominica	Iceland (2)	Nepal (2)
Dominic Rep (3)	Italy (**)	Okinawa (Japan)
Ecuador (3)	Liechtenstein	Pakistan (3)
El Salvador (3)	Luxembourg	Philippines (3)
Grand Cayman	Majorca (Spain)	Rhodes
Grenada	Malta	Singapore (3)
Guatemala (4)	Monaco (2)	Sri Lanka
Haiti (3)	Netherlands (2)	Taiwan (4)
Honduras (2)	Norway (**)	Thailand (2)
Jamaica	Portugal	Turkey
Mexico (**)	Sardinia (France)	
Nicaragua (3)	Scotland	
Panama (3)	Spain (4)	
Paraguay	Sweden (**)	
Peru (4)	Switzerland (**)	
Puerto Rico	Vatican City	
United States **	Wales	
Venezuela (3)		

(**) = Five, or more visits
TOTAL COUNTRIES VISITED (January 2016) = 106

APPENDIX TWO: COUNTRIES VISITED

AFRICA	OCEANA
Algeria	Australia
Angola	New Zealand
Beuchawanaland (Botswana)	
Cameroon, East	
Cameroon, West	
Egypt (4)	
Ghana	
Kenya	
Liberia	
Malawi	
Morocco (2)	
Mozambique	
Nigeria	
Rhodesia (Zimbabwe)	
Swaziland	
Tanzania	
Togo	
(**) = Five, or more visits	
TOTAL COUNTRIES VISITED (January 2016) = 106	

APPENDIX THREE: EMPLOYMENT

Approx. Ages	Employer	Duty
9,10	Various farmers	Picked beans - Ludington - Stayed at cousin Bob Peterson's farm three miles east of Ludington*
11,12,13	None	Collected scrap metals and sold to Cadillac junk dealers (defense and war effort)** Kool Ade stands.
11	Grand Rapids Press:	Paper boy. 40 papers from downtown Cadillac to all customers south of Cobbs Street.** Supervisor - Ed Gallagher
12	Magazine sales	Sold magazines door-to-door in Cadillac; Life, Ladies Home Journal, Colliers, Saturday Evening Post, etc.**
12	Cadillac Evening News	Paper boy. Cooley School area.**
13	LaFranier's Orchards	Picked cherries at a Traverse City area farm. Cooley School Troop #28 Boy Scout project.*
14	Present's Style Shop	Stock boy and janitorial duties in women's apparel shop, downtown Cadillac.** Boss - Louis Present
15	Wooley's Drug Store	Soda fountain (limited) and janitorial duties and customer services, downtown Cadillac.** Bruce Wooley
15 - 18	Cadillac Recreation Dept.	Cadillac Youth Recreation Ass'n. (Program development, maintenance, desk clerk, etc.) ** (Old YMCA Bldg.) Boss - Ed Babcock
15 - 20	Cadillac Recreation Dep't	Life guard and water safety instructor, Community Beach, Lake Cadillac* Boss - Ed Babcock
15 - 20 & 24 - 28	Caberfae Winter Sports	National Ski Patrol**
16	State forest service	Fought forest fires occasionally. (Wartime - fire fighters desperately needed)**
20-24	US Navy	Aerial photographer. Served mostly in Key West, Pensacola and aboard aircraft carrier, USS Tarawa.
25	Oldsmobile Corp	Installed heaters on the final assembly line at the large Lansing plant.*
26	Caberfae Winter Sports	Helped cut down trees and clear land for ski runs.*
28	Frankfort MI High School	Social studies teacher and head coach in football, basketball, track. Sup: Ed Richter

APPENDIX THREE: EMPLOYMENT

Approx. Ages	Employer	Duty
27, 28	Cadillac Junior High School	Science and general mathematics teacher. Head JV and assistant varsity football coach. Director of Cadillac School Camp on Lake Mitchell both summers. Sups: Byrd & Gelston
29	Cadillac Public Library	Drove bookmobile throughout rural areas in Wexford county. Distributed books and showed movies.*
30 - 32	Nub's Nob	Ski instructor and assisted with lay out of runs.**
30 - 32	Harbor Springs Schools	Guidance director and counselor. Taught social studies. Super: Lee Van Hoven
30	Little Harbor Club	Desk clerk and receptionist. Billing. * Boss: Jesus Santos
31	Parker's Dairy	Peddled milk and dairy products to exclusive Wequetonsing summer estates.*
32-36	Western Michigan Univ. Reg. & DA	Admissions Counselor and financial aid director. Student recruitment, admission decisions, foreign student admissions, etc. Friend Russ Gabier recruited me for a changed life! C. Maus
37-45	U. Mich Asst. Dir. Of Admissions	Assistant Director of Admissions. Student recruitment, foreign student admissions, etc. Dir. of Adm. Clyde Vroman
45-60	U. Mich. Director of Admissions	Managed staff of approx. 50. Reported to several VPs
61	Self	Some consulting, secondary and higher education.
62-66	Univ. of Southern Calif.	Dean, Admissions and Financial Aid. Provost: Neal Pings Managed staff of 150
67-68	Academy For Educational Development	Created course numbering and admissions plans for Universidad Automous de Pueblo, Mexico. 12 trips.
67-	Self	Consultant. Among clients were Univ. Wisc., AACRAO, Univ. of Illinois, Edu. Cred. Eval.
	Self	Extensive volunteer work with the International Baccalaureate and the Nat. Coll. Ath. Ass'n (NCAA.)** Wexford Cty. Hist. Society

- *Summer Work Experiences
- ** Part-time Work Experiences

APPENDIX FOUR: RESIDENCES

Year(s)	Address	City/State*
1928 - 30	11830 Ward Street	Detroit
1931	Boon Rd.	Cadillac
1932 - 1946	723 Wood St. (later -South Mitchell St.)	Cadillac
1946 - 1948	Keeler Union Hall, Central Mich. Col.	Mt. Pleasant
1948	Great Lakes Naval Training facility	Great Lakes, Illinois
1948 - 1950	Boca Chica Naval Air Base - Photo lab	Key West, Florida
1950 (6 mos.)`	Pensacola Naval Air Base	Pensacola, Florida
1950 - 1952	USS Tarawa, CV 40	Boston, Mass.
1952 -1953	College Avenue	Mt. Pleasant
1952 - 1953	Delta Sigma Phi House	Mt. Pleasant
1953	Maple Grove Trailer Park	Midland
1954	Trailer Park, Mission Rd.	Mt. Pleasant
1954 -1955	M-22 at Crystal Lake	Frankfort
1955	400 E. Cass St.	Cadillac
1956 - 1957	305 E. Mason St.	Cadillac
1957 -1958	Grant St.	Ann Arbor
1958 -1959	280 West Bluff Drive	Harbor Springs
1959 -1960	313 (?) Third St.	Harbor Springs

APPENDIX FOUR: RESIDENCES

Notes
First home. Very small
Shared farm home with Aunt Pearl and Uncle Bill Hillard
Tree-lined. Brick roadway.
First two years at CMCE. Room 106
Navy "Boot" camp
Included seven months at Pensacola, FL in USN Aerial photographer school
Aerial Photographers training.
Included extended cruises to the Mediterranean Sea and the Caribbean Sea
Junior year at CMU. Roomed with B. Oliver and G. Thompson - one semester
One semester. I was a charter member of the fraternity, joining in 1947.
Married. Senior year at CMU (1st sem)
Graduated from CMU (2nd. Sem.)
Taught and coached at FHS. Cabin on Killian's property on the lake.
Taught in Cadillac. Summer at Cadillac School Camp (Torenta)
Taught in Cadillac. Summer at Cad. Sch. Camp (Home owner)
MA at U of M. Last two months room on Elm St.
Counselor and teacher at HSHS
Counselor and teacher at HSHS

APPENDIX FOUR: RESIDENCES

Year(s)	Address	City/State*
1960 - 1964	1429 Turwill Lane	Kalamazoo
1964	613 Third St.	Ann Arbor
1965 - 1988	2885 Renfrew St.	Ann Arbor
1988 - 1989	1027 South Long Lake Rd.	Traverse City
1989 - 1993	788 E. California Blvd. Apt. #2	Pasadena, California
1993 - 2001	1027 S. Long Lake Rd.	Traverse City
1998	7602 Lakeside Village Dr., Unit G	Falls Church, Virginia
2001	7813 Mackinaw Trail	Cadillac
2004 - 2005	3583 Worth Circle	The Villages, FL
2001 - 2014	7774 Mackinaw Trail	Cadillac
2014 -		Cadillac
		Michigan unless otherwise noted.

APPENDIX FOUR: RESIDENCES

Notes
Admissions work, Western Michigan University
Admissions, U of M. Temporary quarters while new home was being constructed.
New development near Thurston Elementary School (Home owner)
On Long Lake, midway between Traverse City and Interlochen (Home owner)
Dean of Admissions and Financial Aid, Univ. of Southern California. (Home owner)
Retirement home until May, 2001 (Home owner)
May / June. Temporary while I managed AACRAO office in Wash. DC
May 1 - September 1, 2001. Temporary rental home in motel complex.
Not happy there! Very happy with the profit! upon selling. (Home owner)
Near the 17th green of McGuire's golf course.(Home owner)
Two blocks from childhood home.at my old swimming hole.(Home owner)

APPENDIX FIVE: AUTOS OWNED

Car	Bought	Model	Color	Model
Oldsmobile	1952	1947	blue	coupe
Ford *	1955	1955	red	station wagon
Plymouth	1955	1932	grey	4-door sedan
Chevrolet	1960	1958	beige/brown	station wagon
Nash Rambler*	1961	1962	beige	station wagon
Oldsmobile *	1965	1965	white	F-85
Volkswagen *	1967	1968	red	Bug
Plymouth *	1970	1970	green	station wagon
Volkswagen *	1973	1973	red	Rabbit
Oldsmobile *	1977	1978	green	Cutlass Supreme
Toyota *	1982	1982	White	Tercel
Honda *	1986	1986	slate gray	Accord
Chevrolet	1988	1986	red/gray	Blazer 4-wheel
Pontiac	1989	1986	blue	6000
Subaru	1989	1988	red	GL
Dodge*	1993	1994	red	Sports Van
Jeep	1997	1997	black	Utility - 4wd
Chrysler *	1999	1999	white	Town & C. Van
Toyota*	2004	2004	blue	Corolla Sedan
Chrysler*	2006	2006	Silver	Town & C. Van
Chevrolet*	2014	2015	Green	Equinox

APPENDIX FIVE: AUTOS OWNED

NOTES
The "Blue Beetle." 1952 to 1956 College, wedding trip
A true "lemon." Exhaust system replaced every 6 mos. Never again a Ford!
John Dillinger car "look-a-like. Bought as second car for $100 and sold a year later for $100
Bought from Dad's friend in Boyne. Big and good. Great family car.
Little, not much power. Hardly moved in New Mexico windstorm.
Not a bad auto. Bad dealership in Ann Arbor.
A fun car. Took entire family on trips to Cadillac. In accident. No serious injuries.
A perfect car for family approaching and in teen-age years. Good service.
A major disappointment. Not a very good auto.
Maybe our best car, so far. 100,000 plus miles. Saw it on the road in 1991.
An A to B car. Sig bought it from us and drove it until 1991
Good car, but not automatic. A summer car only in 1990 - 1993
Had for less than a year. Undersized engine. Good northern car.
A car for a "little old lady from Pasadena." Comfortable and few
A Japanese junk heap. Major repairs required. For commute Pasadena to USC.
Loaded - Great for trips. Seven passenger. Kept over five years - good resale.
All of the "bells and whistles" Poor gas mileage.
LX Grand. Seven pass - bucket seats. Security syst. Great for trips.
Sky roof, all safety features, 35 to 40 mpg. Very comfortable and fun to drive.
Stow-away & heated seats. Touring model. Leather interior. Our best car!
Crossover, rear view camera. Beautiful shade of green. Sirius radio

APPENDIX SIX: VITA

Cliff Sjogren   *Vita*   620 South Lake Street
                                                                 Cadillac, Michigan 49601

Education

1946	High School Diploma: Cadillac (Mich.) High School
1954	B.S. Degree - Secondary Education: Central Michigan University
1958	M.A. Degree - Guidance & Counseling: University of Michigan
1972	Ph.D. Degree - Guidance & Counseling/International Educ.: University of Michigan

Military

1948 - 1952 U.S. Navy Aerial Photographer. Served in Eastern U.S, The Caribbean, Atlantic and Mediterranean Sea Areas

Major Work Experiences (1954 - 1993)

1954 - 1955	Teacher - social studies - and head coach (Frankfort, Mich. High School)
1955 - 1957	Teacher - science and mathematics - and coach (Cadillac, Mich. Junior High School)
1958 - 1960	Teacher - social studies - and counselor (Harbor Springs, Mich. High School)
1960 - 1964	Admissions Counselor - Western Michigan University, Kalamazoo, Michigan
1964 - 1973	Assistant Director of Admissions - The University of Michigan, Ann Arbor, Mich.
1973 - 1988	Director of Admissions - The University of Michigan, Ann Arbor, Michigan
1988 - 1989	Independent consultant (higher and secondary education)
1989 - 1993	Dean, Admissions and Financial Aid, University of Southern California
1993 -	Sjogren Educational Services (higher and secondary education consulting service)
1994 - 1995	Consultant, *Universidad Autonoma de Puebla* (Mexico): Set up course numbering system and admissions process.
1998	Interim Executive Director of AACRAO (May and June) during search process.
1999	Consultant – Univ. of ILL, Springfield (Create freshman admissions program)
2000	Consultant – Educational Credential Evaluators, Inc. – Office procedures

Lesser Work Experiences (1937 - 1960)

1937 - 1940	Paper routes (Grand Rapids Press and Cadillac Evening News)
1940 - 1948	At various times, fought forest fires, picked beans and cherries, sold magazines
1942 - 1943	Louis Present's Dress Shop (Cadillac) Stock boy
1943 - 1944	Wooley's Drug Store (Cadillac) Stock boy and soda fountain
1944 - 1946	Cadillac Youth Recreation Assoc. - activities, counter, maintenance
1944 - 1948	Swimming instructor and lifeguard - Community Beach, Cadillac
1953 (summer)	Installed auto heaters at Oldsmobile Assembly plant, Lansing
1954 (summer)	Cleared timber to construct ski runs at the Caberfae Ski Area
1955 (summer)	Drove Bookmobile in rural Wexford County, Cadillac Public Library

1956 and 1957 (summers) Director of Camp Torenta (Cadillac School Camp, Lake Mitchell)
1958 (summer) Desk clerk, Little Harbor Club, Harbor Springs, MI
2001 (summer) Delivered dairy products, Wequetonsing summer homes. Harbor Springs

Professional Activities

The American Association of Collegiate Registrars and Admissions Officer (AACRAO)

1963 -	Member of AACRAO
1963 -	Participated as a speaker, panelist, and responder at numerous national, regional, and state meeting
1964	Presented proposal to Michigan AACRAO for a Foreign Credential Review Committee (proposal accepted)
1965	Chairman - MACRAO Foreign Credential Review Committee
1965 - 1969	Member, AACRAO Foreign Credential Review Committee (Chairman - 1967 - 1969)
1966 - 1969	Coordinator, World Education Series publications
1966 - 1973	Member, MACRAO/MASSP Secondary School- College Relations Committee
1974 - 1975	AACRAO Representative to the U.S. Department of State Bureau of Educational and Cultural Affairs
1974	Member of AACRAO Committee that authored the guidelines for the implementation of the Family Educational Rights and Privacy Act of 1974 (Buckley Amendment)
1976	Appointed AACRAO's representative to the Steering Committee for the National Project for Vietnamese and Cambodian Educational Document Evaluation
1976 - 1979	Served AACRAO as Vice President for International Education
1976 - 1979	AACRAO representative to the National Council on the Evaluation of Foreign Educational Credentials
1976 - 1979	AACRAO representative to the Joint Committee on Workshops
1976 - 1979	AACRAO representative to the National Liaison Committee on Foreign Student Admissions
1976 - 1979	Represented the AACRAO Executive Committee at numerous state and regional meetings of the Association
1976 - 1978	Member of AACRAO/IIE/NAFSA Task Force on Data Collection
1976 - 1983	Member of AACRAO/AID Advisory Committee
1979	AACRAO Representative to the International Communication Agency
1979	AACRAO Officers Handbook Committee
1979 - 1988	AACRAO Representative to the National Collegiate Athletic Association (NCAA)
1980	President-Elect of AACRAO
1981	President of AACRAO
1982	Immediate Past President of AACRAO
1988	Awarded the Distinguished Service Award, AACRAO's highest recognition, Awarded Honorary (Life) Membership in AACRAO and MACRAO

National Association for Foreign Student Affairs (NAFSA)

1962 -	Member of NAFSA
1962 -	Participated as speaker, panelist, and respondent at numerous state, regional, and national meetings.
1962	Coordinator of Regional Admissions Activities

1963	Steering Committee for the formation of the NAFSA Admissions Section
1964	Presented formal request for the formation of the Admissions Section to the NAFSA Board (accepted).
1965	Project Director and Philippines Resource person for the First Workshop on the Admission and Placement of Asian Students in U.S. Colleges and Universities, Honolulu, Hawaii.
1965 - 1970	Admissions Section Executive Committee (Chair - 1968-69)
1967 - 1968	Member of the Publications Committee
1968 - 1969	Member of NAFSA Board of Directors
1970 - 1972	Member of Conference Site Committee
1975	Assisted in the preparation of Statement of Principles for Foreign Student Admissions
1977 - 1979	Advisory Liaison representative to the American Council on Education Commission on Collegiate Athletics
1979 - 1980	Member of Commission on Standards and Practices
1988	Awarded Honorary Life Membership in NAFSA

AACRAO // NAFSA Joint Committee on Workshops (JCOW)

1964	Helped draft proposal for formation of JCOW
1965	Director, First JCOW Workshop, Honolulu, (Philippines, India, Japan, Taiwan)
1969 - 1973	Chairman of the Joint Committee on Workshops (JCOW)
	Led JCOW workshops to Scandinavia, and Germany.

FOREIGN TRAVEL

OVERSEAS SCHOOL PROJECT: A College Board project sponsored by the US Department of State.
These assignments consisted of visiting U.S. secondary schools to confer with counselors, headmasters, students, and parents and advise them on current U.S. admissions practices and procedures. U.S. embassies were also visited. Member, the Overseas School Project Committee (1978 - 1988)

1974	Philippines, Japan, Singapore, Thailand, Hong Kong, Taiwan
1975	Japan, Taiwan, Hong Kong, Philippines, Indonesia, Singapore, Malaysia, Thailand, Korea
1976	Hong Kong, Philippines, Taiwan, Japan
1977	Indonesia, Singapore, Malaysia, Thailand, Hong Kong
1978	Argentina, Bolivia, Chile, Paraguay, Peru
1980	Colombia
1981	Jamaica, Haiti, Dominican Republic
1981	Guatemala, Honduras, Costa Rica
1982	Haiti, Jamaica
1983	India, Egypt, Greece, Rhodes
1984	Greece, Egypt, Jordan, Israel
1985	Sri Lanka, Pakistan, Nepal, Greece, India
1986	Greece, Israel, Morocco, Cyprus, Spain, Jordan
1987	Ottawa, Canada
1988	Jordan, Israel, Egypt, Morocco, Spain, Greece, Kuwait

1989	Peru, Bolivia, Paraguay
1993	Pakistan, India, Bangladesh, Nepal, with follow-up visits in London and Rome

B) *Joint Committee on Workshops (JCOW)*

1972	Administrative Director, German/American Workshop on Educational Exchange, Bad Godesberg, Germany
1972	Visited Sweden, Norway, and Denmark to discuss plans for a Scandinavian Workshop on Admissions
1972	Presenter at Workshop on Caribbean Educational Systems on Belize held at Santo Domingo, Dominican Republic
1973	Visited Sweden, Finland, Denmark, and Norway to plan for Scandinavian Workshop
1973	Administrative Director of Scandinavian Workshop on Admissions (visited Norway, Iceland, Denmark, Sweden)
1984	Project Director and principle report author on update of JCOW Workshop, Norway

C) *Other foreign travel*

1965	Fulbright Lecturer (Philippines). Also visited Taiwan, Hong Kong, and Japan
1966	Interviewed and selected students in Kenya, Tanzania, Botswana, and Swaziland under the African Scholarship Program of American Universities (ASPAU), Also visited Malawi, Rhodesia, and Mozambique
1966	Interviewed and selected students in British Honduras, Guatemala, Nicaragua, Costa Rica, El Salvador, and Panama under the Latin American Scholarship Program of American Universities (LASPAU)
1968	Interviewed and selected students in Ghana, Nigeria, and West Cameroon under the ASPAU
1971	Consulted in Peru, Chile, and Ecuador for the National Liaison Committee/U.S. Department of State Project of Foreign Educational Consultations /Workshops.
1972	Visited Belize as a member of the Michigan/Belize Partners of the Alliance Education Team
1974	Youth For Understanding (YFU) consultant to Norway
1977	U.S. Department of State (Iran Desk) consultant to the Ministry of Science and Higher Education, Government of Iran. Evaluated student placement services. Visited officials in Teheran and Isfahan - February.
1977	Returned to Iran to follow up project described above. Visited Teheran, Isfahan, and Shiraz (November)
1977	Visited Germany as member of U.S. Team on German/American Degree Equivalencies.
1978	Visited Germany as guest of FRG to discuss with German officials the admission of "third world students"
1979	Represented AACRAO at the Conference of University Administrators of the United Kingdom, Edinburgh, Scotland
1979	Represented the U.S. Department of Education at the UNESCO (OECD) meeting in Paris, France to discuss international degree equivalencies
1980	Visited U.S. Department of Defense Schools (DODDs sponsorship) in Spain, Italy and the Azores

1981	Represented AACRAO at the Conference of University Administrators of the U.K., Loughborough, England
1982	Reviewed college information centers in Caracas and Maracaibo, Venezuela under sponsorship of the U.S. Information Agency (USIA)
1989	Consulted and conducted admissions workshops in Tel Aviv and Athens
1990	Visited six U.S. Department of Defense high schools in Japan and Okinawa as a consultant on college admissions
1992	Visited five U.S. Department of Defense Schools (DODDs Project) in England,
1993	Visited six U.S. Department of Defense Schools (DODDs Project) in Germany
1993	Participated in USC team visit flown on a private jet to Tokyo, Japan; Taipei, Taiwan; Jakarta, Indonesia; Singapore; Hong Kong; and Seoul, Korea.

Other Significant Activities

1963 - 1968	Committee member and participant of the AACRAO/CEEB/IIE/NAFSA Workshops on Foreign Student Admissions
1965 - 1973	Member, National Council on the Evaluation of Foreign Educational Credentials (Chair 1971 - 1973)
1967 - 1974	Member of the Board of Trustees of the African Scholarship Program of American Universities (ASPAU)
1967 - 1969	Member, ASPAU Selection and Referral Committee
1968 - 1970	National Liaison Committee on Foreign Student Admissions
1968 - 1973	Michigan Partners of the Alliance Committee (Michigan and British Honduras - Belize)
1969 - 1971	Executive Committee of Phi Delta Kappa (Professional Educational Fraternity) - President in 1971, University of Michigan Chapter
1973 - 1976	Member Advisory Council on Test of English as a Foreign Language. Vice Chair,1975-1976.
1973 - 1980	Member Advisory Committee on International Education, College Board. Vice Chair 1975 - 1977 Chair 1978- 1980
1973	Member, Steering Committee on Student Exchange Program for Placement of German Students in U.S. Colleges
1974	Director of Wingspread Colloquium, "The Undergraduate Foreign Student: Institutional Priorities for Action"
1975 - 1978	Member of U.S. Team for the German-American Degree Equivalency Project
1976	Chairman, Test of English as a Foreign Language (TOEFL) Committee on Research
1976 -	Member, Board of Trustees of the International Baccalaureate of North America. Served as member and chair of the IBNA School and College Relations Committee
1979 - 1988	Member, Academic Testing and Requirements Committee of the National Collegiate Athletic Association (NCAA).
1984 - 1988	Chair, Academic Requirements Comm., National Collegiate Athletic Association
1979 -	Member and Chair, NCAA Special Committee on Foreign Student Records.
1980	Appointed NCAA representative to the American Council on Education Special Committee on Intercollegiate Athletics
1980 - 1993	Member, Board of Trustees and Executive Committee of the Indochinese Evaluation Center, Long Beach, California (Wrote Mission and Goals Statement)

1980 -	Served on several scholarship selection committees, Educational Testing Service
1981	Presented testimony to a Congressional Committee on House Bill 1662, "Educational Testing Act of 1981. Testimony later prepared for a syndicated news release.
1981	Member of a committee that drafted the A.C.E. self-regulation initiative guidelines for colleges and universities, "Academic Integrity and Athletic Eligibility"
1981 - 1985	Central Michigan University Alumni Board of Trustees
1982	Wrote original draft of NCAA proposal #48 (Eligibility of freshman student-athletes)
1983	Member N.C.A.A. Special Committee on Academic Research
1983	Consultant, National Commission on Excellence in Education (College Admissions)
1985	Joint Committee of MACRAO, MASSP, State Board of Education members to study Advanced Placement Program for Michigan high schools
1986 - 1988	Faculty, UNC/College Board Institute on College Admissions, Chapel Hill
1987 - 1989	Selection Committee- National Merit Scholarship Program, Evanston
1988 -	Honorary Member, Overseas School Project Committee

Selected Publications

"Academic Success of Hong Kong Students in U.S. Colleges and Universities," Asia Foundation grant. NAFSA. Mimeographed, 1963.

"The Admission and Academic Placement of Students from Nordic Countries: A Workshop Report" (editor). NAFSA, Washington, D.C., 1973. 104 pp.

"Diversity, Accessibility, Quality: A Brief Introduction to American Education for Non-Americans". The College Board, 1977. 36 pp.

"Who's Who Among American High School Students," (contributing editor), Northbrook, Illinois, 1976.

"College Admissions: A View from the Inside". International Quarterly March 1984, pp. 18-21.

"The Changing College Admissions Scene". The Bulletin of the National Association of Secondary School Principals vol. 67, No. 460, Feb. 1983, pp. 1-18. Condensed and printed in the "Educational Digest", Sept. 1983, pp. 28-31.

"Norway: A Guide to the Admission and Academic Placement of Norwegian Students in North American Colleges and Universities". The College Board. (with L. Kerr) A PIER (Projects for International Education Research) Project. 1985, 92 pp.

"Athletics and Academics: A Better Balance Ahead". The Journal of the Michigan Association of Secondary School Principals., Vol. 25, No.1, Fall 1983, pp. 56-58.

College Admissions and the Transition to Postsecondary Education. A paper prepared for the National Commission on Excellence in Education. ERIC Document (1983).

"Diversity, Accessibility, Quality: A Brief Introduction to American Education for Non-Americans". The College Board, (an update of the 1977 pub.), 1986. 45 pp.

Timber Town Tales, History of early Cadillac and Wexford County. Sold 1,000 books first year. All profits contributed to the Wexford County Historical Society. Appeared three times as best seller Northwestern Michigan and twice as second best (paperback non-fiction) by Traverse City Record Eagle paper

Personal

    Military: Served as a US Navy aerial photographer (9 / 1948 to 9 / 1952) Honorable discharge.
    Rotary International (Ann Arbor, Cadillac, and Traverse City clubs): Member since 1975
    Interests: Alpine / Nordic skiing, Writing, travel, classical music, racquet and water sports
    Married: Four grown and married children, eight grandchildren.

Current: Family, travel, cycling, Alpine skiing, volunteer work for, member of Save the Lake group (Cadillac, MI,) created and lead a local memoirs writing group, various local clubs and organizations.
    Volunteer Activities after retirement: International Baccalaureate board and school authorization visits throughout the US, Canada, and the Caribbean area; Friends of the Library; Shepherds Table; President of the Wexford County Historical Society and museum (scanned and written descriptions of more than 1,500 historically significant photos and entered them on our website (www.wexfordcountyhistory.org) Presented more than 50 narrated slide shows Wexford County audiences. Dozens of articles on our area's early history have been published in the Cadillac News (2014.) Wrote best-selling "Timber Town Tales." So far, nearly 1,000 sold.

APPENDIX SEVEN: SPORTS / ACTIVITY HISTORY

air hockey	handball	ski jumping
archery	hide and seek	skiing Alpine
badminton	hiking	skiing Nordic
baseball	hockey, ice	skiing, water
basketball	horseback riding	skijoring (by auto)
bicycling	horseshoes	sledding
board games	hunting, deer, birds, ducks	snorkeling
boating	ice fishing	snowball fights
bocce ball	kayaking	snowshoeing
bowling	kickball	soccer
boxing	kites	softball
Boy Scouts	marbles	squash
camping	model airplanes	stamp collecting
canoeing	paddleball	surfboarding
cards	photography	swimming / diving
caroms	piano lessons	table tennis (ping-pong)
checkers	pickleball	tag
chess	pinball	tennis
croquet	playground apparatuses	tinikling (pole dance)
dancing	pool and billiards	tobogganing
darts	racquetball	track and field
dodge ball	sailing	tree climbing
fishing, sea, lakes, streams	scuba diving	tubing on rivers
foosball	shuffleboard deck and table	volleyball
football	skating, ice	wiffleball
Frisbee	skating, roller	wrestling
golf	skeet shooting	